LANGSTON
HUGHES

LANGSTON HUGHES

❧

Jack Rummel

Senior Consulting Editor
Nathan Irvin Huggins
Director
W.E.B. Du Bois Institute for Afro-American Research
Harvard University

CHELSEA HOUSE PUBLISHERS
New York   Philadelphia

Editor-in-Chief   Nancy Toff

Executive Editor   Remmel T. Nunn

Managing Editor   Karyn Gullen Browne

Copy Chief   Juliann Barbato

Picture Editor   Adrian G. Allen

Art Director   Giannella Garrett

Manufacturing Manager   Gerald Levine

Staff for LANGSTON HUGHES

Senior Editor   Richard Rennert

Associate Editor   Perry King

Editorial Assistant   Laura-Ann Dolce

Copy Editor   Gillian Bucky

Associate Picture Editor   Juliette Dickstein

Picture Researcher   Emily Miller

Senior Designer   Laurie Jewell

Production Coordinator   Laura McCormick

Cover Illustration   Alan J. Nahigian

Creative Director   Harold Steinberg

3   5   7   9   8   6   4

Library of Congress Cataloging in Publication Data

Rummel, Jack.
    Langston Hughes.

    (Black Americans of achievement)
    Bibliography: p.
    Includes index.
    1. Hughes, Langston, 1902–1967—Biography—Juvenile
literature.   2. Poets, American—20th century—Biog-
raphy—Juvenile literature.   [1. Hughes, Langston, 1902–
1967.   2. Poets, American.   3. Afro-Americans—Biog-
raphy]   I. Title.   II. Series.
PS3515.U274Z775   1988   818′.5209   [B]   [920]
87-10920
ISBN 1-555-46595-1
    0-7910-0201-2   (pbk.)

Grateful acknowledgment is made to Alfred A.
Knopf, Inc., for permission to reprint the following
poems by Langston Hughes: "The Negro Speaks of
Rivers," "When Sue Wears Red," "I, Too, Sing
America," "Harlem," and "The Weary Blues" from
Selected Poems of Langston Hughes, copyright © 1959
by Langston Hughes; "Christ in Alabama" from *The
Panther and the Lash: Poems of Our Times,* copyright
© 1932 by Langston Hughes.

CONTENTS

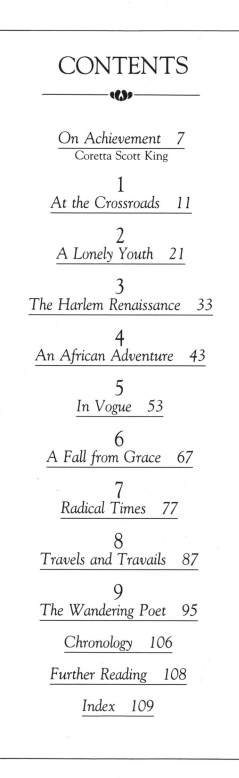

BLACK
AMERICANS
OF
ACHIEVEMENT

MUHAMMAD ALI
heavyweight champion

RICHARD ALLEN
*founder of the
African Methodist
Episcopal church*

LOUIS ARMSTRONG
musician

JAMES BALDWIN
author

BENJAMIN BANNEKER
*scientist and
mathematician*

MARY MCLEOD BETHUNE
educator

BLANCHE K. BRUCE
politician

RALPH BUNCHE
diplomat

GEORGE WASHINGTON CARVER
botanist

CHARLES WADDELL CHESTNUTT
author

PAUL CUFFE
abolitionist

FREDERICK DOUGLASS
abolitionist editor

CHARLES R. DREW
physician

W. E. B. DUBOIS
educator and author

PAUL LAURENCE DUNBAR
poet

DUKE ELLINGTON
bandleader and composer

RALPH ELLISON
author

ELLA FITZGERALD
singer

MARCUS GARVEY
black-nationalist leader

PRINCE HALL
social reformer

WILLIAM H. HASTIE
educator and politician

MATTHEW A. HENSON
explorer

CHESTER HIMES
author

BILLIE HOLIDAY
singer

JOHN HOPE
educator

LENA HORNE
entertainer

LANGSTON HUGHES
poet

JAMES WELDON JOHNSON
author

MARTIN LUTHER KING, JR.
civil rights leader

SCOTT JOPLIN
composer

JOE LOUIS
heavyweight champion

MALCOLM X
militant black leader

THURGOOD MARSHALL
Supreme Court justice

ELIJAH MUHAMMAD
religious leader

JESSE OWENS
champion athlete

GORDON PARKS
photographer

SIDNEY POITIER
actor

ADAM CLAYTON POWELL, JR.
political leader

A. PHILIP RANDOLPH
labor leader

PAUL ROBESON
singer and actor

JACKIE ROBINSON
baseball great

JOHN RUSSWURM
publisher

SOJOURNER TRUTH
antislavery activist

HARRIET TUBMAN
antislavery activist

NAT TURNER
slave revolt leader

DENMARK VESEY
slave revolt leader

MADAME C. J. WALKER
entrepreneur

BOOKER T. WASHINGTON
educator

WALTER WHITE
political activist

RICHARD WRIGHT
author

ON ACHIEVEMENT

Coretta Scott King

BEFORE YOU BEGIN this book, I hope you will ask yourself what the word excellence means to you. I think that it's a question we should all ask, and keep asking as we grow older and change. Because the truest answer to it should never change. When you think of excellence, perhaps you think of success at work; or of becoming wealthy; or meeting the right person, getting married, and having a good family life.

Those important goals are worth striving for, but there is a better way to look at excellence. As Martin Luther King, Jr., said in one of his last sermons, "I want you to be first in love. I want you to be first in moral excellence. I want you to be first in generosity. If you want to be important, wonderful. If you want to be great, wonderful. But recognize that he who is greatest among you shall be your servant."

My husband, Martin Luther King, Jr., knew that the true meaning of achievement is service. When I met him, in 1952, he was already ordained as a Baptist preacher and was working towards a doctoral degree at Boston University. I was studying at the New England Conservatory and dreamed of accomplishments in music. We married a year later, and after I graduated the following year we moved to Montgomery, Alabama. We didn't know it then, but our notions of achievement were about to undergo a dramatic change.

You may have read or heard about what happened next. What began with the boycott of a local bus line grew into a national movement, and by the time he was assassinated in 1968 my husband had fashioned a black movement powerful enough to shatter forever the practice of racial segregation. What you may not have read about is where he got his method for resisting injustice without compromising his religious beliefs.

He got the strategy of nonviolence from a man of a different race, who lived in a distant country, and even practiced a different religion. The man was Mahatma Gandhi, the great leader of India, who devoted his life to serving humanity in the spirit of love and nonviolence. It was in these principles that Martin discovered his method for social reform. More than anything else, those two principles were the key to his achievements.

This book is about black Americans who served society through the excellence of their achievements. It forms a part of the rich history of black men and women in America—a history of stunning accomplishments in every field of human endeavor, from literature and art to science, industry, education, diplomacy, athletics, jurisprudence, even polar exploration.

Not all of the people in this history had the same ideals, but I think you will find something that all of them have in common. Like Martin Luther King, Jr., they all decided to become "drum majors" and serve humanity. In that principle—whether it was expressed in books, inventions, or song—they found something outside themselves to use as a goal and a guide. Something that showed them a way to serve others, instead of living only for themselves.

Reading the stories of these courageous men and women not only helps us discover the principles that we will use to guide our own lives, but it teaches us about our black heritage and about America itself. It is crucial for us to know the heroes and heroines of our history and to realize that the price we paid in our struggle for equality in America was dear. But we must also understand that we have gotten as far as we have partly because America's democratic system and ideals made it possible.

We still are struggling with racism and prejudice. But the great men and women in this series are a tribute to the spirit of our democratic ideals and the system in which they have flourished. And that makes their stories special, and worth knowing. ✤

LANGSTON HUGHES

1
AT
THE
CROSSROADS

GLINTING IN THE last rays of sunset, the train slows as it approaches East St. Louis, Missouri. As the staccato, tapping sounds of the train wheels slow to a steadier beat, a young man sitting at the window of the train watches the small dramas of town life in 1920 unfold before him: a chocolate-colored man, hands in pockets, trudges home at the end of a long day's work in a factory; children in brightly colored clothes shout excitedly as they play a ball game in a rutted street; two women sit on the stoop of their apartment building, talking quietly.

Soon the train is at the edge of the city and begins to climb onto a river bridge. As the young man stares out the window at the choppy waters of the huge Mississippi River, he thinks about how the flow of his own life links him to the people he has just been watching. He pulls an envelope from his pocket and picks up his pen, and on the envelope he begins writing a poem that he calls "The Negro Speaks of Rivers":

Hughes's visit to Mexico in 1920 marked the start of his literary career. While taking in Mexico's sights and sounds, he wrote the poems that were to become his first published pieces. The appearance of these poems in early 1921 was soon followed by the publication of "The Negro Speaks of Rivers," his first fully mature literary work.

Carrie Hughes often left her son in the care of relatives and family friends during much of his childhood. This helped to create in Langston a sense of loneliness and isolation.

I've known rivers:
I've known rivers ancient as the world and older
    than the flow of human blood in human veins.

My soul has grown deep like the rivers.

I bathed in the Euphrates when dawns were young.
I built my hut near the Congo and it lulled me to
    sleep.
I looked upon the Nile and raised the pyramids
    above it.
I heard the singing of the Mississippi when Abe
    Lincoln went down to New Orleans, and I've
    seen its muddy bosom turn all golden in the
    sunset.

I've known rivers:
Ancient, dusky rivers.

My soul has grown deep like the rivers.

Langston Hughes wrote this now-celebrated poem during the summer of 1920, at a time when he was approaching a crossroads in his life. Having just graduated from high school at the age of 18, he understood that his adolescence was quickly drawing to a close and that the time was coming for him to make his way in the world. Yet he felt as though there was no one he could count on for support or advice.

Just as Langston was traveling alone on a train across America, so had he been forced to go through most of his life on his own. Shortly before he was born, his father left his mother and went abroad. His mother then left Langston to be raised by his grandmother and family friends while she searched for work. She returned to take care of Langston only when an opportunity allowed her to stay with him.

Langston got to know his father even less well than he knew his mother. He and his father first met in 1907, when Langston was five years old and his family was briefly reunited in Mexico. He and his father next met 12 years later, when Langston's father, who was traveling from New York City to his home in Toluca, Mexico, wrote to his 17-year-old son, who was living in Cleveland, Ohio: "You are to accompany me to Mexico for the summer." This surprising summons pleased Langston, who immediately looked forward to spending time with a father whom he did not know well and often romanticized about. He dreamed that his father, who had become a successful businessman, was "a kind of strong, bronze cowboy, in a big Mexican hat, going back and forth from his business in the city to his ranch in the mountains."

Yet Langston's vacation in Mexico that summer did not turn out to be a pleasant one. His father proved to be cold and disagreeable rather than kind and wonderful. Racing from one business appointment to another, he paid little attention to his son except to insist that he take up accounting, a subject for which Langston had neither the aptitude nor the desire. Langston felt so overwhelmed by his father's coldheartedness and badgering that he wrote to his mother, "I began to wish I had never been born— not under such circumstances."

However, when the following summer arrived, Langston felt that he had little choice but to turn once more to his father. Having just completed high school, Langston realized that if he was to get ahead in the world, he would need help from someone— and his father was the only person he knew who had enough money to be of any help. Langston's mother, who had returned to Cleveland to live with Langston while he was still in high school, was insisting that he remain with her after his graduation. Her second marriage had failed, and by staying in Cleveland, Langston could help support her and her stepson, Gwyn.

But Langston had his own plans for his future, so he was not anxious to fulfill his mother's wishes even

James Hughes refused to support his son's literary ambitions, urging him instead to pursue a more practical course by studying mining engineering.

Not only were Hughes's first poems published while he was in Mexico, but four of his prose pieces and a one-act play were published by Brownies' Book *as well.*

though he sympathized with them. He realized that what she wanted would mean the end of his schooling. Furthermore, it would mean the end of his chance to experience the larger world beyond the Midwest, where he had grown up.

Having spent most of his childhood without anyone taking very much interest in him, Langston was unwilling to make an extreme sacrifice for someone else. He was also unwilling to make such a sacrifice for his family because he had decided that he was to become a poet. He had been elected class poet when he was in the eighth grade, and at the graduation ceremonies at the end of the school year he had recited a poem he had written for his classmates and fellow students. The enthusiastic applause that followed his reading had made a huge impression on him. "That was the way I began to write poetry," he said. Having received little attention or encouragement while he was growing up, he enjoyed hearing the audience's approval and realized that if he continued to write poems, he could receive additional praise.

Possessing the single-mindedness that any artist must have if he wants to be a success, Langston became determined to strike out on his own and devote himself completely to his education and his art. His plan for accomplishing this was a bold one. It consisted of convincing his father to pay for his college costs at Columbia University in New York City, where Langston wished to continue his studies. A college education from such a prestigious institution would go a long way toward ensuring his success as a well-respected poet.

As Langston journeyed from Cleveland to St. Louis in 1920 and headed toward another reunion with his father in Mexico, he tried to remain hopeful that his father would agree to spend the money. Because his father had not been around to help him in the past,

Langston reasoned, he might be interested in helping him prepare for the future. Despite having a mean nature, his father had shown himself to be a very practical-minded man.

However, Langston's father did not think that his son's plans were very practical at all. Shortly after Langston arrived in Mexico, his father told him that he would not be sent to Columbia in the fall. For a black man to pursue a career as a poet was foolish, according to his father. He could never manage to make a living as a writer.

Langston's father proposed an alternative plan. First, Langston would work for a year in Mexico. He would then go to college abroad, in Switzerland or Germany, to study mining engineering. Once Lang-

James Hughes envisioned a great future for his son in Mexico, but Langston chose to follow plans of his own making.

Jessie Fauset, the editor of Brownies' Book *and a coeditor with W. E. B. Du Bois of* Crisis, *encouraged Hughes early in his career. Fauset was an author in her own right and became the most published black woman of the Harlem Renaissance.*

ston's studies were completed, he would return to work in Mexico—and not in the United States. His father explained that because Langston was black, he would not have a chance to amount to anything in America. But in Mexico, where racial prejudice was not nearly as strong as it was in the United States, he could live a good life and become rich.

Hearing that his future had already been mapped out for him (although not as he had planned it), Langston refused to be manipulated so easily by his father. He promptly found work in Toluca, teaching English in a private school in the morning and giving lessons at a business college in the afternoon. These jobs not only freed him from his dependence on his father, but also enabled him to begin saving a bit of money—not, however, nearly enough to enroll in Columbia later that summer.

Instead of sending himself to New York in September, Langston decided to send three poems he had written during the summer to *Brownies' Book*, a newly established magazine for black children, whose offices were located in New York City. Jessie Fauset, the editor of the magazine, replied to Langston in early October that she wanted to publish one of them, making it the first of his poems to achieve widespread publication. Fauset also asked him to send her other poems and stories he had written.

Within a few months, Langston saw several of his poems, a short play, an essay, and some short stories published in *Brownies' Book*, as well as in *Crisis*, a companion magazine aimed at a black-adult audience. Published by the National Association for the Advancement of Colored People (NAACP), *Crisis* was edited by Fauset and W. E. B. Du Bois, an influential educator and author who headed a small but growing group of black artists and intellectuals based in Harlem, New York. These men and women were in the process of creating a revolution in black art,

The Brownies' Book

MARCH, 1920

BROWNIES LAND.

Hughes was on his way to becoming a well-known writer after one of his poems was published in Brownies' Book in 1920. The magazine was one of a growing number of literary and artistic forums for blacks.

Scholar, author, and civil rights activist W. E. B. Du Bois was a major figure in the struggle for racial equality in the United States. After helping to found the NAACP in 1909, he edited Crisis for 25 years.

thought, and music that came to be known as the Harlem Renaissance. Langston felt encouraged to become a member of this select group in Harlem when *Crisis* accepted "The Negro Speaks of Rivers" in January 1921. But before he could establish himself as a figure in New York's literary scene, he first had to arrive there.

Langston was still based in Mexico half a year later, when the summer of 1921 arrived, yet the time he spent outside the United States proved to be of longstanding value to him. Having learned to speak Spanish, he traveled to Mexico City on weekends to see bullfights and to visit friends. He also encountered a new kind of art, which included the paintings of Diego Rivera and David Siquieros and the writings of Carlos Pellicer. This art did not make use of traditional European images and themes, as most contemporary art did. Instead, these Mexican artists examined their own culture in their art. From these artists, Langston learned to look at his own race when he was in search of material about which to write.

Seeing that his son's works were being published on a regular basis by *Crisis*, Langston's father eventually became so impressed by his son's accomplishments that he could not deny his demands. Langston's father offered to pay the costs for Langston's first year in New York if he promised to study engineering at Columbia. Langston agreed to this offer, applied for admission to the school, and was accepted at once.

In late August 1921 Langston boarded a steamship bound for New York from Veracruz, Mexico, a port city on the Gulf of Mexico. Veracruz was hot and humid at that time of the year, and the uncomfortable climate made Langston all the more eager to leave Mexico for New York. As the ship slipped out of the harbor and into the foggy gulf, he could do little but think about the city of New York that awaited him. Another black writer, James Weldon Johnson, had claimed that New York was soon going to be "the greatest Negro city in the world," and Langston looked forward to contributing to that greatness. ✢

The mouthpiece of the NAACP, Crisis offered blacks a place to publish their literature and social commentary.

2

A
LONELY
YOUTH

J AMES LANGSTON HUGHES was born on February 1, 1902, in Joplin, Missouri. He was named James, after his father, but this name was eventually dropped and he became known as Langston. The only child of James and Carrie Hughes, he never knew what it was like to belong to a happy, closely knit family.

James and Carrie Hughes had been unhappy with one another from the beginning of their marriage, and the reasons for their unhappiness had as much to do with the color of their skin and the society into which they had been born as they did with their opposite personalities. Like most blacks who grew up in 19th-century America, they were victims of white attitudes and discriminatory laws. But in James Hughes's case, being subjected to racial prejudice did not make him feel bitter toward whites so much as it caused him to develop a great deal of contempt for most members of his own race.

The feeling of contempt increased after James Hughes and his wife moved to Oklahoma from Kentucky in the late 1890s. A well-educated man, Hughes taught school in Oklahoma while he studied for the bar exam. His plans for the future were to practice law and buy land. However, these hopes were soon dashed when the state of Oklahoma barred blacks from taking the exam.

Although the institution of slavery was officially abolished in the United States in 1865 with the passage of the 13th Amendment, racial discrimination persisted, and segregation was very much in evidence to Hughes throughout his youth.

Hughes was sent to live with his maternal grandmother, Mary Langston, in Lawrence, Kansas, after his parents were separated. He maintained, "I was unhappy for a long time, and very lonesome living with my grandmother."

Although James Hughes was angry at white society for denying him a chance to pursue his chosen profession as well as his basic civil rights, he chose to blame his own race even more for these injustices. He believed that rather than being the victims of oppression, blacks lacked ambition and therefore were responsible for their status as second-class citizens. This kind of spiteful thinking made James Hughes a hard and bitter man. He seemed to feel hatred for everyone, including himself.

In temperament, Langston proved to be the opposite of his father. Whereas his father was bitter, Langston was easygoing and understanding, especially when it came to his feelings toward other blacks. Yet his courteous and gentle-hearted nature could not prevent him from falling victim to a lonely childhood.

After Langston's parents were separated, his mother left him for long periods of time while she moved from city to city in search of work. During these periods he lived mostly in Lawrence, Kansas, with his grandmother, Mary Langston, who was about 70 years old when Langston first started to live with her. She was a strong-willed woman who was fiercely opposed to racial discrimination, and she tried to protect her grandson from discrimination of any kind. Accordingly, Langston learned from her to fight racial prejudice, but he also lived a sheltered life when he was under her care.

While Langston was growing up, he also stayed occasionally in Lawrence at the home of some family friends, James ("Uncle") and Mary ("Auntie") Reed. "For me," Langston said, "there have never been any better people in the world. I loved them very much." Although the Reeds, like his grandmother, treated him well, their kindness could not make up for a lack of affection from his parents. Living with his grandmother and the Reeds in all-white neighborhoods, Langston often felt even more isolated. And as he grew older, several experiences away from his home compounded his feeling of loneliness.

When Langston was ready to start going to school in 1908, his mother was told that because her son was black, he could not attend a nearby, chiefly white school in Topeka, Kansas. He would have to go to a school for black children across town. Langston's mother fought with the school board over this decision. Since she worked every day, she argued, she was unable to bring Langston to a school that was so far away and he was too young to travel through the

Carrie Hughes won her fight in 1908 to have her son admitted to the mostly white Harrison Street School in Topeka, Kansas. According to Hughes, "My mother . . . was always ready to do battle for the rights of a free people."

Hughes lived briefly in Topeka with his mother in one room on the second floor of this building.

streets of the city by himself. Carrie Hughes won her argument, and Langston was allowed to enter the first grade of the nearby school.

Once in school, Langston was made to sit in a far corner of the classroom, at the end of the last row. He came to feel so isolated in school that he was removed from class by his mother before the year had ended.

When a similar situation occurred six years later, Langston had grown old and bold enough under his grandmother's guidance to fight back. After he and his black classmates were moved into a separate row, away from the white children, he wrote up signs that said "Jim Crow Row" (a reference to then legally permissible discriminatory practices against blacks known as Jim Crow laws). He gave a sign to each black student to put on his or her desk. This led to Langston's being expelled from the school. A protest from a group of parents over the teacher's discrimination got Langston reinstated, and separate seating for blacks and whites was no longer allowed.

Fortunately, neither of these experiences affected Langston's desire to learn. Throughout his life, he remained an exceptionally eager and able student, excelling wherever he studied.

Langston's sense of isolation reached a climax when he was 12 years old. He was taken to church by Auntie Reed to experience the feeling of being "saved" by Jesus. As the church service progressed, the members of the congregation came forward one by one and announced that Jesus had entered their hearts. This meant that their souls had been purified by contact with God.

Eventually, all the members of the congregation except Langston came forward to say that they had been saved. Langston had not felt anything, and he did not want to pretend that he had. Yet the congregation waited for him to come forward, and Auntie

Reed prayed for him. To escape from the unbearable pressure that he felt was being placed upon him, Langston announced at last that he, too, had been saved. His pronouncement made the congregation shout with joy.

Later that night, after everyone in Auntie Reed's house had gone to bed, Langston broke down and cried. He said:

> That night, for the last time in my life but one—for I was a big boy of twelve years old—I cried, in bed alone, and couldn't stop. I buried my head under the quilts, but my aunt heard me. She woke up and told my uncle I was crying because the Holy Ghost had come into my life, and because I had seen Jesus. But I was really crying because I couldn't bear to tell her that I had lied, and I had deceived everybody in the church, that I hadn't seen Jesus, and that now I didn't believe there was a Jesus any more, since he didn't come to help me.

Unlike the girl shown here, Hughes failed to experience the religious fervor that led to one's being "saved." This failure left him disillusioned with religion and intensified his feelings of loneliness.

John Brown's raid on the United States arsenal at Harper's Ferry, Virginia, in 1859 heightened tensions just before the start of the Civil War. The abolitionist Brown captured the arsenal, but federal troops retook it the next day.

One of the ways that Langston sought to overcome his loneliness was by losing himself in a private world of stories. His grandmother, wearing her first husband's bullet-riddled shawl (which had been in his possession when he was killed in John Brown's raid on Harper's Ferry just before the start of the Civil War), recounted to Langston how his forebears had fought against slavery. "She sat, looking very much like an Indian in her rocker," he said, "and read the Bible or held me in her lap and told me long beautiful stories about people who wanted to make Negroes free."

Another way in which he attempted to deal with his feelings of loneliness was by writing poetry. Requiring that he take a good, hard look at himself as well as at the world around him, writing enabled him to let out his feelings and express what he felt.

Langston's love for the written word prompted him to become a frequent visitor to the library in Lawrence. The atmosphere of the library held a certain mystique for him. "The silence . . . the big chairs, and long tables, and the fact that the library was always there and didn't have . . . any sort of insecurity about it—all made me love it," Langston said. "I believed in books more than people."

Langston also loved the theater, along with what was then the newest invention in American culture, the motion picture. His mother, who had wanted to be an actress, took him to the theater when he visited her in Kansas City, and the theater came to hold the same attraction for him that it did for her. But the movies never quite attracted him as much as the theater did, for his grandmother was outraged that the cinemas in Lawrence had a policy of racial segregation, and she forbade him to see any more movies.

When Langston's grandmother died in 1915, he went to live with his mother, her second husband, Homer Clark, and Clark's two-year-old son, Gwyn. Langston's new family moved to wherever Clark could find work. They went from Lawrence, Kansas, to Kansas City, Missouri, to Lincoln, Illinois. With every move, it seemed more and more as though Langston did not have a true home—until his family arrived in Cleveland, Ohio, in the summer of 1916. Langston enrolled in Cleveland's Central High School and attended classes there for four years.

Soon after the family moved to Cleveland, Clark began to feel that his marriage to Carrie was failing, and he left abruptly for Chicago, Illinois. Langston's mother took Gwyn and followed her husband to Chicago, hoping for a reconciliation. Langston was left in Cleveland all by himself, forced to care for himself in an attic room that he rented in someone's house. "I couldn't afford to eat in a restaurant, and the only thing which I knew how to cook myself in the kitchen

Hughes's grandmother often told him stories about slavery and freedom. He said, "Through my grandmother's stories always life moved, moved heroically toward an end."

Hughes with some of his friends at Central High School in Cleveland, Ohio, where he came into contact with an ethnically diverse student body.

where I roomed was rice. . . . Then I read myself to sleep," he said. His mother and Gwyn returned to Cleveland to live with him nearly two years later, in the spring of 1919.

To make up for his unstable home life, Langston devoted himself to his classwork and to other interests as well. He participated in a number of extracurricular activities while he attended Central High. Besides joining the editorial staff of the school magazine, known as the *Monthly*, he was elected to the student council, he was a standout member of the school's track team, he was an officer in the drill corps, and he acted in school plays.

Central High proved to be a good place for Langston to go to school. One of the oldest and most distinguished secondary schools in Cleveland, it had traditionally been the school where Cleveland's white elite—including John D. Rockefeller, the great financier and philanthropist—had been educated. However, by the time Langston arrived at Central High, its student body was more ethnically diverse than it had been in the past.

Waves of immigrants had recently hit the northern industrial states as people came looking for work from eastern and southern Europe as well as from the southern United States. Because very little industry was taking place in Europe while World War I was being fought there, the industrial North sought to increase its productivity. Cities such as Cleveland attracted people from all over the globe.

Langston's best friend in high school was Satur Andrzejewski, a young man whose family had emigrated from Poland. Several of Langston's other friends, who worked with him on the *Monthly*, were from Jewish families that had come from eastern Europe and Russia. Langston's Jewish friends at Central High made an especially lasting impression on him, for they were the ones who first introduced him to the ideas of socialism.

Socialism is the doctrine that all property in a society is public property. This property is then divided among the people in the society so that all men and women share equally in the fruits of each other's labors. This concept appealed to Langston partly because he did not have very much he could call his own and partly because he wanted every man and woman to be treated fairly and equally. He began to read socialist magazines such as the *Socialist Call* and the *Liberator,* as well as books by authors with politically radical points of view, such as John Reed's *Ten Days That Shook the World,* which describes the Russian Revolution in 1917. Claude McKay, a black writer whose articles and poems appeared in the *Liberator,* became a particular favorite of Langston's.

While Langston was reading these authors, he had reason to believe that he, too, had a talent for writing. During his four years at Central High, he wrote a number of poems and short stories for the *Monthly.* Many of his early poems reveal an unpolished beginner searching to find his poetic voice, but Langston gradually began to understand what kind of poetry he wanted to write. He composed a number of poems about social injustice that made use of free verse rather than a traditional verse form such as the sonnet. These poems show the influence of the favorite poets of Langston's youth, Carl Sandburg and Walt Whitman.

In other poems Langston began to employ Negro dialects as well as the words and rhythms of the music he had heard when he was taken to black churches and Sunday school by Auntie Reed. In still others he sought to capture either street talk or the music known as the blues. The mournful, lonely sound of the blues held a special appeal for Langston.

Walt Whitman's unconventional free-verse style of poetry strongly influenced Hughes's early writings.

An example of Langston's evolving style can be seen in a poem that he wrote to a high school sweetheart, a young black girl who had recently moved to Cleveland from the South. The poem is called "When Sue Wears Red."

When Susanna Jones wears red
Her face is like an ancient cameo
Turned brown by the ages.

Come with a blast of trumpets,
Jesus!

When Susanna Jones wears red
A queen from some time-dead Egyptian night
Walks once again.

Blow trumpets, Jesus!
And the beauty of Susanna Jones in red
Wakes in my heart a love-fire sharp like a pain.

Sweet silver trumpets,
Jesus!

Hughes's poetry began to reflect images of black experience—also captured here in Romare Bearden's "After Church"—as well as black dialects and sounds as he developed his identity as a member of the black community.

In this poem, Langston compares Sue's beauty with the classic beauty of an ancient cameo and an African queen, and echoes his comparisons with the delighted, religious cries of "Jesus!" Combining images from ancient and modern times, the poem is a celebration of all black beauty.

Most of Langston's early poems focused on how it felt and what it meant to be black. Because several members of his family—particularly his grandmother—had a history of championing black rights, Langston was well acquainted with the problems that confronted blacks. He often felt a bit removed from other blacks while he was growing up because he lived in all-white neighborhoods and went to mostly white schools. However, the sounds and music of black culture attracted him, and his father's hostility toward blacks managed to draw Langston even closer to them. Above all, he could identify with their sense of feeling alienated from the rest of society. Having no specific family to whom he could feel close, he ultimately sought to embrace all of black society in his poetry.

Langston's strategy of capturing black sights and black sounds would serve him particularly well in the days to come, when he would settle in the mostly black community of Harlem, New York. ❧

When Hughes moved to Harlem in 1921, the district was in the process of becoming the most heavily populated black residential area in the United States.

3

THE
HARLEM
RENAISSANCE

❧

Hughes ARRIVED in New York City by steamship on the evening of September 4, 1921. The city's famous skyline dazzled the 19 year old. "There is no thrill in all the world," he said, "like entering, for the first time, New York harbor—coming in from the flat monotony of the sea to this rise of dreams and beauty. New York is truly the dream city." After helping some of his fellow passengers find their way around New York, he took a subway uptown, to 135th Street in Harlem, and rented a room at the Harlem YMCA.

Harlem in the 1920s was the largest and most influential black community in the United States. Not only was it a center of black intellectual life, but it was an artistic center as well. Hughes ached to plunge headlong into this stimulating neighborhood, but he had an obligation to fulfil: he had to attend Columbia University. Accordingly, after staying for a few days at the Harlem YMCA, he paid a visit to the Columbia housing office to secure a dormitory room for himself.

During the time that Hughes was entering college, most universities made it very hard for blacks to gain admission. The few blacks who were admitted

Harlem in the 1920s "became the symbol of liberty and the Promised Land to Negroes everywhere," according to clergyman Adam Clayton Powell, Sr.

33

to such universities usually had to live in segregated dormitories or else find private housing off campus. In this respect, Columbia University was no different than other universities. Hughes had difficulty in getting a dormitory room even though he had applied for and had been granted one in advance. He finally talked a housing officer into letting him have a room on campus, and he became the only black student during that year to live in a university dormitory.

He enrolled in a standard course of freshman studies: English, French, contemporary civilization, physical education, and physics. His classes, however, did not interest him (the mathematics taught in the physics course that his father insisted he take was completely beyond him). He preferred to indulge himself in his love for the theater.

During Hughes's first year in New York, he attended the hit Broadway musical of the season, Eubie Blake and Noble Sissle's *Shuffle Along*. The play fea-

Hughes's year of study at Columbia University in New York was not an especially happy one for him, as life at the Ivy League school offered its share of troubling racial encounters.

tured the singer Florence Mills and—for one of the first times on a Broadway stage—an all-black cast. He also saw Eugene O'Neill's *The Hairy Ape* and *Anna Christie*, George Bernard Shaw's *Mrs. Warren's Profession*, a production by a theater group from Moscow, and a number of other plays.

Several months into the fall semester, Hughes received a letter from Jessie Fauset, his editor at *Brownies' Book* and *Crisis*. He had been so shy about meeting the well-known editors of *Crisis* that he had not yet told them that he had moved to New York. But once Fauset found out that he was in town, she invited him to meet her and W. E. B. Du Bois at the offices of the NAACP (Du Bois had cofounded the National Negro Committee, which later became the NAACP). Hughes accepted her invitation. Accompanied by his mother, who had come to see him in New York, he met Fauset, Du Bois, and other members of the *Crisis* and NAACP staffs. This was an important meeting for Hughes; it was his initial introduction into a circle of people who would influence black thought in 20th-century America.

Fauset was impressed enough with Hughes to offer him a standing invitation to visit her home in Harlem. Others who attended this meeting were equally impressed. Augustus Granville Dill, the business manager of *Crisis*, invited Hughes to spend his Christmas vacation at Dill's apartment. Accompanied by Dill and other *Crisis* workers, Hughes subsequently attended concerts and lectures, and he dined at the few private clubs in New York that were open to black membership.

While leading a full cultural life in New York, Hughes managed to achieve good grades at Columbia. At the end of the first semester he had a B-plus average. However, he was becoming more and more dissatisfied with his life as a student at a prestigious Ivy League school. White students kept him at a cool

Musician Eubie Blake, shown here at age 95, was one of the popular performers whom Hughes went to see during his first years in New York.

Hughes said of his generation, "We build our temples of tomorrow, strong as we know how, and we stand on top of the mountain, free within ourselves."

distance; his only real school friend was a Chinese student from Honolulu. Hughes wanted to write for the school newspaper, the *Spectator*, but the only assignment that was given to him was to write a column covering the white fraternities. Because he was black and no one in the fraternities would talk to him, it was an impossible assignment to fulfill.

Langston's father was grudgingly sending his son money to pay for that first year in New York, as he had promised he would do. However, he demanded to know how Langston spent the money and how he was doing in school. When he found out that Langston had not made A's in all of his subjects, he threatened to stop sending money. Eventually he relented, and Langston received $300—enough to pay for an overcoat and expenses to last through the winter.

In May 1922, Hughes received word that his father had suffered a stroke and was critically ill. By this time Hughes had made up his mind to spend more time on his poetry and to leave Columbia. He also wanted to spend more time in Harlem. There, he said, "Everybody seemed to make me welcome," which was not how he was treated at Columbia.

Hughes wrote to his father to inform him of this decision and to return the latest check that had come to him from Mexico. When he received no reply after a month, he wrote another letter, then another. He finally received a reply from his father's housekeeper that his father's health was improving, and then stopped writing to him altogether.

After finishing the spring term, Hughes moved to Harlem and tried to find a job. He answered ad after ad in the newspapers, only to be told by his would-be employers that they were looking for whites only. At last he found a job as a laborer on a vegetable farm outside the city. It was hard work, and it did not leave him any time to write, but Hughes was content to have a break from mental labor for a while.

By early September, the growing season was over and the workers were let go. Hughes next worked for a florist, but then, tired of low-paying, city-bound jobs, he searched along the docks of New York for work aboard a ship. He landed a job on a freighter called the *Oronoke*, but much to his surprise, the ship was not bound for foreign lands. Instead, it headed up the Hudson River to be put into storage at Jones Point, New York, along with dozens of other freighters that were no longer needed after the end of the World War I.

Despite Hughes's tremendous disappointment at not getting a chance to sail abroad, he decided to stay in upstate New York with the crew that watched over the ships. His life at Jones Point was quiet. The work was light, there was plenty of time to write, and he was regularly given leave, during which time he visited New York and Washington, D.C. He also spent some of his leave with his friend Countee Cullen in Harlem.

According to Hughes, "My youthful illusion that Harlem was a world unto itself did not last very long."

Countee Cullen went from being Hughes's close friend to his chief poetic rival as the two poets differed in their opinions of what it is that their poetry should try to accomplish.

Hughes had spent a lot of his time during his first year in New York at the Harlem branch of the New York Public Library. One of the persons he met there was Cullen, an up-and-coming poet. The two men got along well and traded poems with one another for appraisal and criticism.

Cullen and Hughes approached their poetry in different ways. Cullen was interested in poetry that demanded exact syllable counts and certain sounds to complete a rhyme scheme. Hughes, on the other hand, preferred to write in free verse. Like Cullen, he carefully chose his language so it would fit the subject and emotion of his poems, but his poetry was not so formal in style.

Not only did their poetic styles differ, but the two poets held differing views about the relationship between their race and their poetry. Hughes could not separate his interest in blacks from his desire to write poetry. He wrote about black people, black music, and black experiences while using black American speech rhymes and slang. Cullen considered himself to be a poet first and foremost, a poet who just happened to be black, so he did not center his poetry on his blackness. Instead, Cullen tended to write in a private voice about personal matters. In this way, he was almost the opposite of Hughes, who wrote in a boisterous voice about very public events: lynchings, jazz clubs, bill collectors, and the like. Despite these differences, the two men encouraged each other's work.

Hughes's poems were steadily published throughout 1922. Cullen even read some of them as part of public readings held at the Harlem branch of the public library. Yet Hughes seemed to be struggling in his work. He was searching for a breakthrough that would raise his poetry to a higher level. That breakthrough came one night in March 1923, in a Harlem

blues club, when he began writing "The Weary Blues."
The poem perfectly expressed Hughes's desire to capture black music and speech in his poetry.

> Droning on a drowsy syncopated tune,
> Rocking back and forth to a mellow croon,
>   I heard a Negro play.
> Down on Lenox Avenue the other night
> By the pale dull pallor of an old gas light
>   He did a lazy sway. . . .
>   He did a lazy sway. . . .
> To the tune o' those Weary Blues.
> With his ebony hands on each ivory key
> He made the poor piano moan with melody.
>   O Blues!
> Swaying to and fro on his rickety stool
> He played that sad raggy tune like a musical fool.
>   Sweet Blues!
> Coming from a black man's soul.
>   O Blues!
> In a deep song voice with a melancholy tone
> I heard that Negro sing, that old piano moan—

*Jazz bands such as this one per-
forming at a club in Harlem
helped to inspire Hughes in his
writing.*

Scholar and teacher Alain Locke developed his influential friendship with Hughes by corresponding with the poet in January 1923. The two men finally met in Paris a year and a half later.

"Ain't got nobody in all this world,
Ain't got nobody but ma self,
I's gwine to quit ma frownin'
And put ma troubles on the shelf."
Thump, thump, thump, went his foot on the floor.
He played a few chords then he sang some more—
"I got the Weary Blues
And I can't be satisfied.
Got the Weary Blues
And can't be satisfied—
I ain't happy no mo'
And I wish that I had died."
And far into the night he crooned that tune.
The stars went out and so did the moon.
The singer stopped playing and went to bed
While the Weary Blues echoed through his head.
He slept like a rock or a man that's dead.

What Hughes accomplished in this poem was new and remarkable. His use of rhythm and cadence, imitating black speech and blues music, was a brilliant coup. In writing "The Weary Blues," he took the sounds of street music and street talk and transformed them into a powerful and evocative voice all his own.

Hughes soon learned from Fauset that one of his poems was going to be published in an anthology entitled *Negro Poets and Their Poems*. This anthology was certain to give Hughes exposure to a larger audience. Fauset reminded him, "Hold fast to your dreams. . . ."

Along with Cullen's and Fauset's support, Hughes also received encouragement from Alain Locke. The first black American to win a Rhodes scholarship, Locke had a quick mind and was vastly learned. He was graduated magna cum laude in philosophy from Harvard, received a Rhodes scholarship to Oxford University in England, continued his graduate studies at the University of Berlin and the College de France, and then became a professor at Howard University in Washington, D.C. He wanted to assemble a group of intellectuals and writers who would enliven American culture, and he started to correspond with Hughes at his friend Cullen's suggestion.

In one of Locke's letters to Hughes, he suggested that Hughes, Cullen, and Jean Toomer (another promising young black writer, who was the author of *Cane*) work together on common projects. Hughes responded that he was interested in forming a small literary circle, although at the moment he was more interested in traveling, especially to France. He was becoming restless in Jones Point. Locke suggested that Hughes join him and Cullen on a trip to Europe that summer, but Hughes declined the invitation, preferring to travel on his own.

On June 4, 1923, Hughes quit his job on the Hudson and came to New York to search for a ship that would take him to a distant place. Unlike his first search for work aboard a ship, this time he found what he was looking for. The ship was called the *West Hesseltine*, and its destination was Africa. ❧

"I was in love with Harlem long before I got there," Hughes maintained. *But by the spring of 1923, he had become anxious to visit other places.*

4

AN
AFRICAN
ADVENTURE

THE *WEST HESSELTINE* was not a cruise ship by any stretch of the imagination. It was a rusty, old freighter ready to make the difficult and dangerous voyage to the west coast of Africa. Since the trip would not be an easy one, the captain of the *West Hesseltine* could not be choosy when selecting his crew: He felt lucky to have a crew at all. So when Hughes arrived at dockside with excellent letters of recommendation from his supervisor at Jones Point in hand, he was hired immediately.

The ship left New York on June 13, 1923. Hughes was excited to be on the open sea at last, heading for an exotic foreign land. Although the 1920s marked a time when only the wealthy could afford to travel abroad, Hughes was en route to one of the least-traveled continents of the world.

Africa is considered by many black Americans to be their mother continent. They feel that life there will offer them a kind of freedom that no black in America can know. The belief that Africa is the black homeland and the lost black Eden to which Afro-Americans should return was the major theme of the black-nationalist Marcus Garvey, who founded the first American chapter of the Universal Negro Improvement Association (UNIA) in 1917. The UNIA embraced the slogan "Back to Africa" and attempted to organize blacks who lived in the Western hemisphere in a mass exodus to Africa. The project aroused

During Hughes's visit to Africa in 1923, he was as impressed with the openness of the people there as he was with the wild style of dress.

A champion of black unity, Marcus Garvey was the charismatic leader of the "Back to Africa" movement, which sought to establish a central homeland for blacks.

widespread interest among black Americans, but largely because of the size of the project, it ultimately failed. Hughes was aware of Garvey's activities, along with the efforts of his friend and mentor W. E. B. Du Bois to organize a Pan African Congress. The meeting of this congress consisted of blacks seeking to protest European colonialism in Africa. Neither Garvey nor Du Bois had ever been to Africa. Yet that was where Hughes was going.

During the first night of his voyage, Hughes unpacked his bags in his cabin. He then took the collection of books he had carried with him while he was in New York onto deck. Suddenly, he threw all of the books—except for Walt Whitman's *Leaves of Grass*—into the ocean. As he later wrote:

> It was like throwing a million bricks out of my heart—for it wasn't only the books that I wanted to throw away, but everything unpleasant and miserable out of my past: the memory of my father, the poverty and uncertainties of my mother's life, the stupidities of color-prejudice, black in a white world, the fear of not finding a job, the bewilderment of no one to talk to about things that trouble you, the feeling of always being controlled by others—by parents, employers, by some outer necessity not your own. All these things I wanted to throw away. To be free of.

During the summer of 1923, the *West Hesseltine* made 32 stops up and down the West African coast. Hughes's first impressions of Africa were of its intense heat and the wild styles of dress of the people. Their dress ranged from near nakedness to unusual combinations, such as tribal robes worn with bowler hats. Gradually, Hughes saw through these surface impressions to the more important events that were occurring in Africa.

In Africa, nations did not exist in the usual sense of the term. The continent was a mixture of tribal cultures, although most of the tribes had already been influenced by the colonial powers of Europe, which exercised political control over almost all of the continent. Most of West Africa was divided between the British and the French, although tiny Belgium ruled the huge colony of the Belgian Congo (now, after gaining its independence, called Zaire), and Portugal controlled the vast colony of Angola in southwest Africa.

Africa was not free politically, nor was it free economically. The African people were not allowed by their political masters in Europe to manufacture goods from their own raw materials. Materials such as palm oil, cocoa beans, and mahogany were shipped to Western countries, turned into various products, and then returned to Africa at a high price; the African people were given no jobs in producing these goods.

As the ship made its way slowly down the coast, from Senegal to Nigeria to the Cameroons (where Hughes crossed the equator for the first time and, according to custom had his head shaved by the ship's crew), the tragedies of European colonialism were evident everywhere. The white traders and missionaries who had seized control of parts of Africa worked the African people very hard. Yet, to Hughes's surprise, many Africans still managed to live with a zest and grace that won his immediate respect and empathy.

Another surprise came when Hughes realized that the Africans whom he encountered did not think he was black. "The Africans looked at me and would not believe I was Negro," he said. "They looked at my copper-brown skin and straight black hair and they said: 'You—white man.' "

The voyage provided Hughes with similarly memorable encounters. In Port Harcourt, Nigeria, he met a boy who was the son of a white father and an African mother. The boy, who was light-skinned like Hughes,

For Hughes, his visit to Africa was "the real thing, to be touched and seen, not merely read about in a book."

As Hughes continued to have his poems published in Crisis *through the early 1920s, he developed a steady readership.*

approached him and asked if it was true that people in America would talk to mulattoes like himself. In Africa, the boy explained, mulattoes were ignored by the native population. "He looked very lonely, as he stood on the dock the day our ship hauled anchor," Hughes said. "He had taken my address to write me in America, and once, a year later, I had a letter from him, but only one, because I have a way of not answering when I don't know what to say."

Such meetings benefitted Hughes's writing. He published several short stories inspired by his trip. His poems "The White Ones" and "Dream Variation" were also written as a result of experiences he had in Africa.

The *West Hesseltine* went down the African coast to the Belgian Congo, then steamed up the Congo River for more than 100 miles to take on cargo. The poor Congo villages, with their taverns posting signs that said "Whites Only" and their patrols of armed black soldiers enforcing white colonial rules, depressed Hughes. The ship only remained at dock in the Congo for a few days before heading for Angola, the southernmost stop on the itinerary. The *West Hesseltine* proceeded to retrace its route back up the coast as far as Guinea, then started back home to New York.

With its hold full of African timber, copra (dried coconut meat), and other goods, the *West Hesseltine* returned to New York on October 21, 1923. Hughes was greeted as a returning hero by his friends from Harlem. They told him that an entire page of the August issue of Crisis had been devoted to his poems and encouraged him to take an active part in Harlem's growing literary circle, which was headed chiefly by Fauset.

However, Hughes still wanted to see and know more of the world, so in December he shipped out on the *McKeesport* from Hoboken, New Jersey, to the

Netherlands. Rotterdam was cold and white with snow when he arrived, and Hughes liked the whiteness, the narrow cobblestone streets of the city, and the cozy teahouses. He returned to Hoboken in late January 1924, but when he was offered a return trip to Europe on the *McKeesport*, he took it. He left on his second European voyage a few days later on February 4, 1924.

During the voyage, Hughes thought of leaving the ship once it reached Rotterdam for an extended stay in Europe. When he got into an argument with the ship's steward a few days before they reached Holland, the disagreement helped Hughes to make up his mind. The day after the *McKeesport* landed in Rotterdam, he accepted his advance pay from the captain and used part of it to buy a train ticket to France.

Hughes arrived in Paris possessing only a few dollars and the names and addresses of two people. One of them—Claude McKay, the writer whom Hughes admired when he was a high school student in Cleveland—had just left Paris to live on the French Riv-

"I shall try not to write anything else this summer, as there are so many things to see in Paris," Hughes said during his visit to this European capital in 1924.

iera. The other, a friend of Fauset's named Rayford Logan, told Hughes that he would see if he could find him a job.

Hughes rented a hotel room for his first night in Paris, then spent the next day looking for work at English-speaking establishments—the American Express office, the American library, and the U.S. embassy—without having any success. However, within a few days Hughes finally managed to get himself hired—as a bouncer at a nightclub frequented by prostitutes and their drunken customers. Fights occurred frequently at the club, and when the first one erupted, Hughes fled into the night.

Luckily for Hughes, Fauset's friend Logan soon came through with a job offer, and Hughes was hired as a dishwasher at a popular nightclub, Le Grand Duc. The club was partially owned by an American, Eugene Ballard, who had been the only black pilot to fly in the Lafayette Flying Corps during World War I. The American-type club offered southern-style cook-

Nightclub scenes similar to this one were a familiar sight to Hughes while he worked at Le Grand Duc in Paris.

ing, plenty of wine, and—what made it especially popular with the Parisians—American jazz.

Hughes went to the club every evening at eleven and worked past the closing time, which was three in the morning. From three until the sun came up a floating group of musicians would drift in and out of the club to play in all-night jam sessions. The stars of the club were the singers Florence Jones and Ada Beatrice Queen Victoria Louisa Virginia Smith (known more informally as Bricktop). Pianist Palmer Jones, trumpeter Cricket Smith, and drummer Buddy Gilmore were among the musicians who showed up for the jam sessions.

Shortly after spring arrived in Paris, Hughes met Anne Coussey. Part Scot and part African, she had been educated in England, and she had come to Paris to study French. Hughes was immediately attracted to her, and he soon began spending many of his afternoons at her apartment in the Latin Quarter of Paris. Their relationship proceeded to the point where Coussey asked Hughes whether he would consider marrying her, even though she had received a proposal of marriage from someone in London. Hughes told her that he was not interested in marriage because it would interfere with his life as a poet. Their relationship grew strained after this exchange. Coussey eventually left Paris—and Hughes's life—in the late spring.

Hughes's relationship with Anne Coussey marked the start of a pattern that would recur several times in his life. He would fall deeply in love with a woman, then pull back as his feelings grew deeper and the relationship became more serious. He was never able to overcome his boyhood sense of isolation.

One morning during the summer of 1924, Alain Locke arrived in Paris. He knew through Countee Cullen that Hughes was in the city, and he paid Hughes a visit in order to meet him for the first time

Bricktop, one of the stars who performed regularly at Le Grand Duc while Hughes was working there, displays photographs from the 1920s of songwriter Cole Porter and herself.

European society, which Hughes called "the circus of civilization," offered a powerful contrast to the living conditions that he observed in Africa.

and to present him with two proposals. The first was that Hughes submit some poetry for a special issue on blacks for *Graphic Survey* magazine, which Locke was going to edit. The second was that Hughes travel with Locke to Italy.

Hughes had already been invited to Italy by two Italian brothers who were waiters at Le Grand Duc. Like most business establishments in Paris, the club was closing for the month of August. Hughes arranged to meet Locke in Verona, Italy, after he visited the two brothers.

During Hughes's trip to Italy, he got along well with Locke, who proposed that if Hughes were ever to enroll at Howard University, he should stay with him. Yet as they traveled together, a strain developed in their relationship—one that became apparent when Hughes and Locke were planning to depart for America from the port of Genoa. On the train from Venice to Genoa, Hughes was robbed while he was sleeping. For reasons that have never been made clear, Locke did little to help out Hughes other than lend him a small amount of money. Locke then departed for America while Hughes, stranded in Genoa, was forced to live at a settlement house for down-and-out sailors.

With barely enough money to live on, Hughes kept trying to get a job on a ship bound for America, but he had no luck in getting hired chiefly because he was black. As he saw white sailors find work aboard ships without much difficulty, he become more and more downcast, particularly because he had grown desperate for money. In such a depressed frame of mind, he wrote "I, Too, Sing America," one of his most powerful and best-known poems.

> I, too, sing America.
>
> I am the darker brother.
> They send me to eat in the kitchen
> When company comes,
> But I laugh,
> And eat well,
> And grow strong.
>
> Tomorrow,
> I'll sit at the table
> When company comes.
> Nobody'll dare
> Say to me,
> "Eat in the kitchen,"
> Then.
> Besides,
> They'll see how beautiful I am
> And be ashamed,—
>
> I, too, am America.

The staff of the Crisis *published Hughes's work in their magazine for almost half a century.*

Hughes was finally forced to send a frantic request to the *Crisis* staff in New York for financial assistance. Although the money never arrived, a ship willing to take him on soon did. The ship was the *West Cawthon*, bound for New York and staffed by an all-black crew.

Hughes later explained this harrowing ordeal with characteristic good humor. "The months before," he said, "I had got to Paris with seven dollars. I had been in France, Italy, and Spain. And after the Grand Tour of the Mediterranean, I came home with a quarter, so my . . . European trip cost me exactly six dollars and seventy-five cents!" 🙰

5

IN
VOGUE

─── ❧ ───

HUGHES RETURNED from Europe in November 1924 to discover that the Harlem Renaissance was flourishing. During the 10 months that he had been gone, several black writers—including Jessie Fauset—had been published by major presses, indirectly helping all black writers to gain a wider reading audience. A new magazine, called *Opportunity*, was published by the National Urban League and edited by Charles Johnson. Along with the *Messenger*, which was edited by the labor leader A. Philip Randolph, *Opportunity* gave black writers another prestigious place to publish their work besides *Crisis*.

Chief among the Harlem-based writers who saw their reputations beginning to grow was Hughes himself. Many of his poems, including "Dream Variation" and "Grant Park" were appearing in different magazines and journals. So when Hughes attended a benefit party for the NAACP on the night of his return from Europe, he was greeted warmly and as a well-respected peer by such eminent black writers as Walter White and James Weldon Johnson.

Unlike his first arrival in New York, this time Huges did not think it was so important to be in the middle of Harlem's cultural excitement. In early 1925, he moved to Washington, D.C. He planned to attend nearby Howard University and to be with his mother and stepbrother Gwyn, who were living in the nation's capital.

Taking a job as a busboy at the Wardman Park Hotel ultimately provided Hughes with a valuable boost to his literary career.

Hughes maintained, "An artist must be free to choose what he does, certainly, but he must also never be afraid to do what he might choose."

They were staying with wealthy relatives of Carrie's uncle, John Mercer Langston. Long deceased by the time Hughes moved to Washington, John Mercer Langston had made a name for himself in the Civil War and Reconstruction eras as a clerk of an Ohio township, then as inspector-general of the Freedman's Bureau, the agency created by the federal government to protect ex-slaves after the end of the Civil War. He later was appointed ambassador to Haiti and ended his political career as a congressman from Virginia.

Hughes's Washington relatives were excessively proud people who lived in an elite and exclusive world. Because his mother came to Washington without money or social standing, they treated her with little respect. Hughes was dealt with more carefully by his relatives. He was, after all, an author who was published by respected magazines. Still, he disturbed them with his stories of shipping out on old freighters and washing dishes in Paris jazz bars, for these were activities of which they did not approve. Shortly after Hughes took a job in a steam laundry, he moved with his mother and Gwyn into a rooming house in an unfashionable neighborhood, far from the swank streets where their Washington relatives lived.

Once Hughes had moved to a neighborhood that he found more suitable, he started spending more time at blues clubs and streetcorner joints. Hughes drew inspiration from these places. "I tried to write poems like the songs they sang on Seventh Street," he said. These songs "had the pulse beat of the people who keep on going."

Among the poems that Hughes wrote during this time were "The Cat and the Saxophone" and "Railroad Avenue." With their syncopated sounds and free-form lines, these works were further refinements of Hughes's blues and jazz poetry. Much as a cubist painter will take a realistic, recognizable figure and change it into a series of cubic blocks to indicate depth and movement, so Hughes arranged single words and short phrases on a page to convey a sense of motion and life.

Although Hughes's creative output in Washington was high, he was still doing lowly and unsatisfying labor. After working at the laundry for a brief period, he got a job at an oyster house, and then he was employed as an assistant to Dr. Carter Woodson, the editor of the *Journal of Negro History*. Woodson had received a large grant from both the Carnegie and Rockefeller Foundations to establish a publishing company devoted to the study of Afro-Americans. He hired Hughes to help prepare one of the first volumes of this study entitled *Free Negro Heads of Families in the United States in 1830*. Hughes admired Woodson and his work, but he found his own job of proofreading and alphabetizing 30,000 names to be rather tedious. Nonetheless, he needed the money, so he remained with Dr. Woodson in Washington through most of 1925.

Hughes returned briefly to New York in May 1925 to attend a banquet sponsored by Charles Johnson and *Opportunity* magazine. The banquet was held to give out awards and monetary prizes as part of a literary contest to determine the best black writers in America. The contest was judged by a panel of distinguished American writers and publishers, including Robert Benchley, Eugene O'Neill, and Alexander Woolcott. The contest was divided into different literary categories, and Hughes's main rival in the poetry contest was Countee Cullen, whose work was becoming extremely popular with both blacks and whites.

A star-studded, glittering affair, the awards dinner proved to be an important night for the 23-year-old Hughes. His poem "The Weary Blues," written two years before but still unpublished, won first prize and was read aloud to the banquet audience by James

James Weldon Johnson practiced law before becoming a published author and serving on the NAACP staff in New York. In addition to his poetry and fiction, he wrote numerous songs, including the black anthem "Lift Every Voice and Sing."

Singer and actor Paul Robeson was one of the most recognizable people in America before his Communist sympathies compelled him to leave the country.

Weldon Johnson. Among the people with whom Hughes became acquainted that night was Carl Van Vechten, a writer and critic. One of the few whites in New York to investigate the Harlem that existed outside the white-only jazz clubs (such as the Cotton Club), Van Vechten was intensely interested in the new artistic movements that were developing in New York. A critic whose words appeared in many influential magazines, he had begun to champion various black artists, including the actor and singer Paul Robeson. Van Vechten and his wife also invited black and white artists, writers, publishers, and agents to parties in their home, attempting to bring blacks and whites together in New York.

Over the next two weeks, Van Vechten worked with Hughes on editing his poetry. Then, during a lunch with his own publisher, Alfred Knopf, Van Vechten presented Hughes's poetry to Knopf and recommended that he publish Hughes's work. Knopf quickly agreed. A mere 17 days after the *Opportunity* dinner in New York, Hughes signed a contract for the publication of his first work of collected poems, *The Weary Blues.* Van Vechten wrote the introduction to the book, and the Mexican artist Miguel Covarrubias designed the cover.

Hughes was astonished with Van Vechten's clout. He was also ecstatic. He wrote Van Vechten, "As the old folks say, I'll have to walk sideways to keep from flying."

Yet this was not the end of Van Vechten's promotion of Hughes. Van Vechten wrote articles about black arts and culture for the popular magazine *Vanity Fair* and arranged for several of Hughes's poems to appear in one of its issues. "Never in my wildest dreams had I imagined a chance at Vanity Fair," Hughes said.

Hughes's sudden success in the publishing world created a flurry of excitement among his friends in

Harlem. However, his success did not change the circumstances of his life. He continued to work for Dr. Woodson in Washington, and he still shared the same two-room apartment with his mother and step-brother. He hoped that his publishing success would help him get a scholarship to Howard University, especially because he could no longer depend on the influence of Alain Locke, who had been fired from the Howard faculty because of his involvement in a student strike. Hughes applied for a scholarship to the university but was turned down.

In the fall of 1925, Hughes moved out of his family's apartment and quit his job with Dr. Woodson. Supported by the small amount of money he had received from *Vanity Fair*, an advance payment

Cab Calloway leads his orchestra at the Cotton Club, the most famous of the white-only jazz clubs in Harlem.

Writer and critic Carl Van Vech-ten proved to be a wonderful ally and adviser to Hughes throughout the poet's life.

from his publisher, Knopf, and some money from Van Vechten, he tried for a few months to write an autobiography, something that Van Vechten had encouraged him to do. Hughes lived in a room at Washington's 12th Street YMCA, but the writing went slowly and with difficulty. He was not yet ready to write the story of his life—except as it might appear in his poetry. Worried about his future and wondering whether he would ever return to college, he moved back in with his mother and took a job as a busboy at the Wardman Park Hotel.

Hughes was working in the restaurant of the hotel in late November when Vachel Lindsay, one of America's best-known poets, visited the hotel to give a poetry reading. Recognizing Lindsay in the restaurant from his picture in the morning newspaper, Hughes thought of going over to Lindsay and introducing himself but shyness got the better of him. Instead of saying anything, Hughes "wrote out three of my poems on some pieces of paper and put them in the pocket of my white bus boy's coat. In the evening when Mr. Lindsay came down to dinner, quickly I laid them beside his plate and went away, afraid to say anything to so famous a poet, except that I liked his poems and these were poems of mine."

During Lindsay's reading that night, he announced to his audience that he had discovered a promising young black poet and then proceeded to read aloud all three of the poems that Hughes had left for him. The next day, members of the press surrounded Hughes, photographing him at the hotel in his busboy's uniform and asking him about himself. By the end of the month, the story about Hughes and Lindsay had been picked up by the Associated Press wire service and was carried all over the country. The episode was all the publicity Hughes needed to launch the publication of *The Weary Blues* in January 1926.

Although Hughes's literary career was on the rise, he was still anxious to go to college. Late in October 1925 he had applied and been admitted to Lincoln University, a small, all-black school not far from Philadelphia, Pennsylvania. However, Hughes could not count on attending college until he found enough money to pay for three years of schooling. After attending a November party in his honor at Van Vechten's apartment in New York (a party, he noted, that none of the black leadership in Washington had ever thought to give him), he met Amy Spingarn, the daughter of a wealthy industrialist. Spingarn, her husband, and her brother-in-law were all deeply in-

After taking a number of odd jobs over the years to support himself, Hughes welcomed the opportunity to become a student at Lincoln University in Pennsylvania.

A portrait of Hughes painted by his patron Amy Spingarn around 1930.

volved in the struggle for racial equality in New York; they donated generously to the NAACP and many other black organizations.

Hughes explained to Amy Spingarn that he wanted to finish his university education but that he did not have the money to do so. He further explained that even though most of his friends were urging him to attend an Ivy League school, preferably Harvard, he wanted to go to Lincoln. He described his experiences at Columbia, then told her he was searching for someone who could help him out financially. Spingarn did not make any promises to him, although she did say that she would keep his dilemma in mind. The day before Christmas Hughes received a letter in Washington. Spingarn would underwrite his education. He should choose a school to his liking and enroll immediately. "It was the happiest holiday gift I've ever received," said Hughes. "My poems—through the kindness of this woman who liked poetry—sent me to college."

Hughes entered Lincoln University in February 1926. Along with Lincoln's reputation for academic excellence—the students referred to it as "the black Princeton"—Hughes elected to study there because the school was only a train ride away from New York. Although he worked diligently at Lincoln, he made frequent, and sometimes extended, visits to Manhattan. He did not want to miss out on what he called "the period when the Negro was in vogue."

After Hughes's first semester of school ended, he spent the summer of 1926 in Harlem living in the same apartment building as his friend Wallace Thurman. The two of them headed a group of young black artists who began to spend a lot of time with one another. The other artists in the group included Zora Neale Hurston, a writer and folklorist then studying at Columbia University; the painter Aaron Douglas; actor and writer Bruce Nugent, whom Hughes knew from Washington; and the poet and artist Gwendolyn Bennett, just back from studying in Europe. Hurston called this group the "Niggerati."

Hughes had a fair amount of money coming in that summer—he began to receive royalties for *The Weary Blues*, payment for a magazine article he had written, and the winnings from another poetry prize—so he was able to spend a good deal of the summer concentrating on his poetry. He also devoted a lot of his energy to writing lyrics and scenes for a black musical revue that had been proposed by Caroline Reagan, a friend of Van Vechten's. The play was to be called *O Blues!* and was supposed to star Paul

Writer Zora Neale Hurston stands alongside Hughes during a visit in 1927 to Tuskegee Institute in Alabama.

Hughes with some of his friends in 1927, a year that proved to be one of the happiest in his life.

Robeson. However, Hughes's work on the play was interrupted by his teaming up with Hurston to write the plot, dialogue, and lyrics for a black opera. This project, too, faltered after a while.

The Niggerati did succeed in completing one of their works: the publication of a one-issue magazine called *Fire!!* According to Hughes, it was published to "burn up a lot of the old, dead conventional Negro–white ideas of the past." It was also supposed to counter the reaction of the black bourgeoisie to some of Hughes's earthy blues poems, as well as the critical savaging by middle-class blacks of Carl Van Vechten's new novel, *Nigger Heaven*. Hurston, Hughes, Nugent, and Thurman hoped that *Fire!!* would provide young black artists with a place to publish their work. The magazine was almost not issued because the Niggerati could not raise enough cash to pay their printer. Van Vechten finally loaned them enough money to ensure its publication. The magazine was met with outraged condemnation. "None of the older Negro intellectuals would have anything to do with *Fire!!*" Hughes said. The Niggerati thus succeeded in provoking a response with *Fire!!* but they never managed to put together enough money to print more than one issue.

In the fall of 1926, Hughes was back at Lincoln University, editing and paring his latest poems into a book-length manuscript. When he had finished his editing, he sent the poems to Van Vechten, who submitted the manuscript to Knopf. The poems were published in February 1927 under the title *Fine Clothes to the Jew*. Although protests were made about the title being anti-Semitic, it was actually taken from a poem in the collection that described hard times. In this poem, Hughes sought to make use of the stereotype of Jews as pawnbrokers, people whose services would be in demand when times grew hard.

The poems in *Fine Clothes to the Jew* offered as earthy and unsentimental a description of black life as had then been published. The poems did not present a falsely pretty picture of black life. Several of the characters were drunks and prostitutes. Sex and violence were among the themes incorporated into the poetry. Hughes wrote about the darker side of black life, partly because it attracted him and partly because it existed and so few others had written about it. "My poems are indelicate," he admitted. "But so is life."

Several leading members of the black press attacked *Fine Clothes to the Jew* for presenting a negative view of blacks to the world. The *Amsterdam News* in New York reviewed it under the headline "Sewer Dweller"; the *Pittsburgh Courier* called it "piffling trash." Hughes replied by pointing out that he was not the first to write about such characters. He said, "Solomon, Homer, Shakespeare, and Walt Whitman were not afraid to include them."

In mid-April 1927, a few months after the publication of *Fine Clothes to the Jew*, Hughes met a woman in her seventies who in time would have an important, almost crushing effect on his life. Her name was Charlotte Mason, and she was introduced to him through Alain Locke. The widow of a well-known psychologist and physician, Mason was an heiress to generations of wealth. Her Park Avenue apartment, which afforded a dramatic view of Manhattan, was filled with exquisite collections of European, African, and American Indian art.

Having been told by Locke that Hughes was an up-and-coming poet, Mason summoned Hughes to her apartment to tell him about her hope of fostering black art and writing. She believed that blacks, like Indians, were "primitive people" who were in closer contact with nature and their natural impulses than

Charlotte Mason became Hughes's chief patron in the spring of 1927. Their relationship lasted for three-and-a-half years.

were whites. She insisted that she did not mean this as an insult, but as praise. Her mission, she told Hughes, was to save the world—at least to save those things that were natural and spontaneous in the world—by making the art and writing of blacks better known. "As the fire burned in me," she said, "I had the mystical vision of a great bridge reaching from Harlem to the heart of Africa, across which the Negro world, that our white United States had done everything to annihilate, should see the flaming pathway . . . and recover the treasures their people had had in the beginning of African life on earth." Hughes said of her, "I found her instantly one of the most delightful women I had ever met, witty and charming, kind and sympathetic."

Mason wanted Hughes (as well as Locke and Hurston) to help her realize her vision. She would give him money to support his work, and he would acknowledge her guidance in the direction his work would take. For Hughes, who had been poor all his life, her offer was one he could not afford to turn down.

Hughes's tour of the South after his first semester at Lincoln University took him past isolated scenes much like this one in Tennessee.

In addition to needing financial help, there was something in Hughes's emotional makeup that responded deeply to Mason. Shortly after their first meeting—and after Mason began to be Hughes's patron—she requested that he not call her "Mrs. Mason" but "Godmother." Hughes agreed. He maintained, "No one else had ever been so thoughtful of me, or so interested in the things I wanted to do, or so kind and generous toward me."

After Hughes's first semester at Lincoln ended in May, he left on a tour of the South. He read some of his poems at Fisk University in Nashville, Tennessee, then continued farther south to Memphis, Tennessee, and New Orleans, Louisiana. This poetry-reading tour was the first of many he was to give (in his later years, such tours would become an important way for him to support himself). It was also his first trip to the South. He viewed the trip as an opportunity not only to make some money with his readings, but also to get to know southern blacks better.

From New Orleans, Hughes took a small freighter to Havana, Cuba, for a brief stay. He then returned to New Orleans and started traveling north, stopping off at Mobile, Alabama. Walking down the main street in Mobile, he unexpectedly encountered Zora Neale Hurston, who was driving around the South for the summer, collecting field notes for her mentor, the anthropologist Franz Boas of Columbia University. Hughes and Hurston traveled north together, visiting Tuskegee Institute, founded by Booker T. Washington, in Montgomery, Alabama; rushing over to Macon, Georgia, to catch a performance of the legendary blues singer Bessie Smith; and visiting the isolated, rural black churches.

The summer of 1927 proved to be a rare carefree time for Hughes. In the years that were to follow, he would not have many happy periods like this one again. ❧

Blues vocalist Bessie Smith was admired by Hughes, and her singing helped to inspire his blues-based poetry.

6

A FALL
FROM GRACE

❧

SHORTLY AFTER the fall semester of 1927 began at Lincoln, Hughes traveled to Manhattan to see Charlotte Mason. He was presented with a concrete proposal of financial support that would last for the next three years. He would be paid $150 a month so that he would not have to worry about anything other than his writing. And if he wanted to travel for purposes of literary investigation, she would pay his expenses on top of his regular monthly stipend.

Hughes gratefully accepted Mason's offer. But once he had taken on her support, his life and work began to change. His poetry decreased in both quality and output. Perhaps Hughes had simply exhausted his creative abilities for a while; after all, he had just published two full volumes of poetry, and he was devoting much of his time to a semiautobiographical novel about a lonely, young black boy's passage from childhood to maturity. Yet something else was influencing his work as well. By patronizing Hughes, Mason—no matter how noble her intentions—was helping to deprive the poet of the emotional intensity he needed to produce truly inspired work.

The psychological relationship between Hughes and Mason grew tangled. He developed a deep affection for her that went far beyond mere gratitude

Word of the stock market crash spreads through New York's financial district on October 24, 1929. The crash resulted in economic chaos and hard times for Americans all across the country.

Blues composer W. C. Handy formed a lasting friendship with Hughes, and their collaborations helped the poet to improve the musical quality of his art.

for the financial support she offered. For Hughes, Mason became something like a second mother. The emotional support she gave him—the feeling of being cared for, of not being alone anymore—kept him coming back to her apartment for long afternoons of conversation. Hughes said:

> Out of a past of more or less continued insecurity and fear, suddenly I found myself with an assured income from someone who loved and believed in me, an apartment in a suburban village for my work, my brother in school in New England and no longer a financial difficulty to my mother, myself with boxes of fine bond paper for writing, a filing case, a typist to copy my work, and wonderful new suits of dinner clothes from Fifth Avenue shops, and a chance to go to all the theater and operas and lectures, no matter how expensive or difficult securing tickets might be. All I needed to say was when and where I wished to go and my patron's secretary would have tickets for me.

Growing accustomed to the finer things in life, Hughes saw his enthusiasm for academics decrease during 1927 and 1928. He wrote the lyrics of a song for W. C. Handy, the preeminent blues composer. He authored a few sonnets as well as some mild social protests for the socialist magazine *New Masses*. However, he had to be careful with his poems of social protest. Charlotte Mason hated socialism.

In the summer of 1928 Hughes went into seclusion in a rented apartment near Lincoln and continued working on his novel about a young man coming of age. The story was set in Kansas, where Hughes had spent the earliest part of his childhood. He finished the first draft in the fall and dutifully sent a copy to his godmother. Mason liked parts of the story but urged him to begin a second draft. The revision proved to be a difficult task. Hughes felt uncomfortable when writing long works of fiction, and his godmother's scrutiny inhibited him. During the academic year that began in 1928—his senior year at Lincoln University—he worked on the second draft of the novel as often as his schoolwork and his forays into Manhattan would allow him.

After graduating from Lincoln University in the spring of 1929, Hughes took a room—at Charlotte Mason's urging—in the quiet, residential town of Westfield, New Jersey, which was about an hour's travel from Manhattan. He hired Louise Thompson, who had been married briefly to Hughes's friend Wallace Thurman, to type for him, and he began to work steadily on the novel, without spending as much time as usual in Manhattan.

By then, Hughes's friends in the Niggerati had left Harlem. Bruce Nugent was in London working as an actor, Zora Neale Hurston was in the South working on her field notes for her dissertation, and Wallace Thurman was in Hollywood, trying to earn a living as a writer. They had all seen Harlem change since its glory days only a few years before. Whereas the people who lived in Harlem in the mid-1920s were filled with hope and optimism, by the late 1920s feelings of boredom and weariness had set in. The crash of the New York Stock Exchange on October 24 would add to this somber mood and downward slide and seal Harlem's fate as an economically depressed area.

By the summer of 1929, Hughes was ready to claim, "I've never felt so unpoetic in my life. I suppose I'm not quite miserable enough. I usually have to feel very bad in order to put anything down." He continued with a third revision of the novel, which he named *Not Without Laughter*, through the fall of 1929. He finally finished it just before Christmas, and the novel was published in early 1930.

Admired for its depiction of ordinary black life, *Not Without Laughter* received a tremendous amount of praise. Among its admirers was the *Pittsburgh Cou-*

Hughes often suggested that he felt isolated from people, yet he was regarded by his friends as full of warmth and childlike joy.

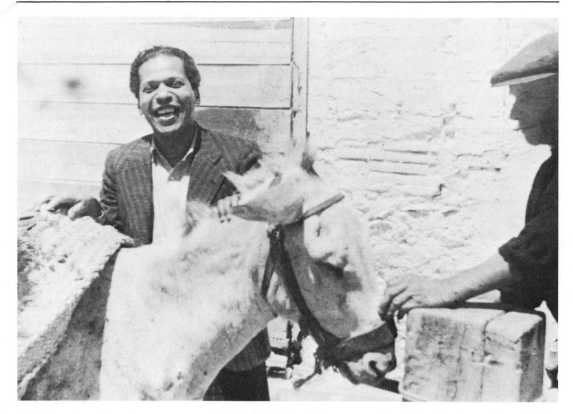

Cuban national poet Nicolás Guillén was greatly influenced in his work by his friend Hughes's poetry.

rier, which had disapproved of Hughes's previous book. The newspaper now stated, "Bring out the laurel wreath and drape the brow of Langston Hughes."

Hughes's next project was to resume work on a folk opera, which he called a "singing play." He began searching for a composer to work with his lyrics but was unable to find anyone suitable in New York. He decided to travel to Cuba, where he could research Afro-Caribbean and Latin American music. Mason thought that doing such research was a wonderful idea and provided him with the money for the trip.

Hughes arrived in Havana in late February, shortly after his 28th birthday, and promptly introduced himself to Jose Antonio Fernández de Castro, the editor of Havana's principal newspaper. Fernández de Castro had translated some of Hughes's poetry into Spanish. Through him, Hughes met a number of the leading young Cuban poets, including Nicolás Guillén, who would soon become famous in the Spanish-speaking world for accomplishing much the same thing that Hughes had done in English: using native rhythms (in Guillén's case, Afro-Cuban rhythms) and speech in poetry while confronting the problems of racism along with European and American imperialism.

Fernández de Castro and Guillén helped Hughes with his "singing play" project by taking him to many of the well-known music clubs in Havana, where Hughes heard the percussive, Afro-Cuban music called *son*. He decided to use this music for his opera, but he still had trouble finding the right person to compose it. He finally gave up on his search for a composer and returned to New York in early March. He felt refreshed from his trip, but he was still without a clear feeling of what he should do next. Charlotte Mason saw to it that he did not have to look far for answers.

Like Hughes, Zora Neale Hurston also had Mason for a patron. At the elderly woman's request, Hurston

After winning the Harmon prize for achievement in black literature, Hughes was able to afford a trip to Cuba and Haiti in April 1931. Here he dines with a group of writers in Havana.

Hughes's two-week tour of the streets of Havana in 1930 resulted in his establishing lifelong friendships with several young Cuban writers.

moved to Westfield, New Jersey, into a house not far from where Hughes lived. Soon the two began working together on a play called *Mule Bone*, based on the myths and folkstyles of rural southern blacks. They had just about finished the play when things started to go very wrong between Hughes and his patron.

The only poems that Hughes was able to complete after his return from Cuba dealt with his feelings of guilt mingled with anger. Thanks to Mason's money, he was able to lead a comfortable life while other's were suffering through the hardships of the great economic depression that followed the stock market crash. Hughes's feelings emerged in poems such as "Advertisement for the Waldorf-Astoria," which parodied an advertisement for the new and socially exclusive Waldorf-Astoria Hotel in New York.

Unable to complete any long-term projects, including his singing play, Hughes began to disappoint

Mason with his lack of productivity. She felt that he was spending too much of his time socializing with Hurston and too little of his time working hard. When Mason told him of her disappointment, Hughes believed that she was trying to exercise control over his writing. He told her, "So far in this world, only my writing has been my own, to do when I wanted to do it, to finish only when I felt it was finished, to put it aside or discard it completely if I chose . . . nobody ever said to me 'you must write now. You mush finish that poem tomorrow. You must begin to create on the first of the month.' " While he resented her attempted increase in authority, she accused Hughes of being ungrateful to her. Much to Hughes's disappointment, their friendship—and their financial arrangement—collapsed.

Depressed at the thought of losing the support of the one person who understood "how I must battle the darkness within my self," Hughes turned to writing despondent poems, such as "Dear Lovely Death":

The luxurious Waldorf-Astoria Hotel, built after the stock market crash, became the target of a scathing, anti-capitalist poem by Hughes.

> Dear lovely Death
> That taketh all things under wing—
> Never to kill—
> Only to change
> Into some other thing
> This suffering flesh,
> To make it either more or less,
> Yet not again the same—
> Dear lovely Death,
> Change is thy other name.

After trying and failing to have a meeting of reconciliation with Charlotte Mason, Hughes finally realized that their relationship was over. In late December 1930 he left Westfield to join his mother in Cleveland. While there, he gave a poetry reading for the students and teachers at his old high school. He also discovered by coincidence that *Mule Bone*, the play he and Hurston had collaborated on, had been copyrighted in Hurston's name only and was being offered as a production for theater groups. Hughes was surprised at Hurston's greediness, and confronted her about her claiming sole credit for the play. He made her agree to a settlement but this incident severed their friendship.

During this struggle with Hurston, Hughes was awarded the Harmon Prize for achievement in black literature. The prize money was a relatively large sum for Hughes, $400, and he used this money to finance a trip in April 1931 to Cuba and Haiti. In Cuba, Hughes visited friends and revived himself under the warm Caribbean sun. He then sailed to Haiti, where he made a pilgrimage to the fortress of La Ferriére, a citadel built atop a mountain in the country's rugged interior. The citadel had been established by the 19th-century revolutionary leaders Toussaint L'Ouverture, Jean-Jacques Dessalines, and Henri Christophe, who were part of a generation of black Haitians who successfully rebelled against Haiti's French colonial rulers. These men had helped Haiti to become the world's first black republic.

The ruins of the fortress and of the Sans Souci palace in the jungle below it represented to Hughes more than just the decline of a mighty black power. The sight of these ruins reminded him of his own fall

Hughes's visit in Haiti to the ruins of the fortress of La Ferrière, a symbol of past black glory, renewed his desire to write.

from grace and affected him deeply. It renewed his sense of purpose. As Hughes put it, "When I was twenty-seven the stock-market crash came. When I was twenty-eight, my personal crash came. Then I guess I woke up."

Although Hughes felt a sense of renewal amid the ruins in Haiti, he was disturbed by some of this black republic's other sights. "It was in Haiti," he said, "that I first realized how class lines may cut across color lines within a race, and how dark people of the same nationality may scorn those below them."

Toward the end of Hughes's stay in Haiti, he met Jacques Roumain, an important innovator in third-world literature. Like Hughes (and Guillén in Cuba), Roumain was using his poetry to explore the folk motifs of his native land. Hughes and Roumain enjoyed one another's company immensely and began a lifelong friendship.

In July, after having been gone from the United States for three months, Hughes left the Caribbean to return to New York. While traveling up the East Coast from Florida to New York, he stopped at Bethune-Cookman College in Daytona Beach, Florida, to meet Mary McLeod Bethune, the college's president. Her suggestion that he give a reading tour of his poems in the South stayed in his mind as he headed north—with the famous educator as an unexpected traveling companion.

Hughes's trip to the Caribbean helped him to gather his thoughts, although it had not left him particularly optimistic that all of the injustices in the world would ever be corrected. For a time he had thought otherwise. While meeting such people as Charlotte Mason, Alain Locke, Zora Neale Hurston, and Wallace Thurman, Hughes had been a man filled with childlike hope and wonder. Now, after weathering some troubled times, he knew that his days of innocence were over. ❧

Educator Mary McLeod Bethune advised Hughes to "go all over the South with your poems. People need poetry."

RADICAL
TIMES

WHEN HUGHES returned to New York from Haiti, in August 1931, the Great Depression was almost two years old and the economy showed no signs of recovery. "Had I started looking for work, a job would have been hard to find. Thousands were out of work," he said. "But I did not want a job. I wanted to continue to be a poet."

Freed from the constraints of his relationship with Charlotte Mason, Hughes became much more politically radical than he had been before. Deeply interested in how the depression was affecting America's middle and lower classes, he formed a close association with the John Reed Club, a group made up mostly of writers and intellectuals who shared his left-wing views of social and political issues. He also began writing for the magazine *New Masses* and became a director of a traveling repertory company called the New York Suitcase Theater. The John Reed Club, the Suitcase Theater, and *New Masses* all had close connections with America's Communist party. Hughes always denied being a member of the party, even though he admired many of the positions the party took on various disputes.

Hundreds of out-of-work men wait in line to register for unemployment relief as the depression takes hold of New York in 1931.

One action taken by the Communist party that earned Hughes's respect was its quick and vigorous defense of nine black youths convicted in the Scottsboro case. Just when Hughes was leaving for Cuba and Haiti in March 1931, the youths had been arrested and nearly lynched in Alabama for allegedly raping two white women. All of the people involved in the case—the alleged victims as well as the alleged assailants—had been riding illegally on a train, where the crimes were said to have taken place. Although the evidence against the accused young men was weak, an all-white jury found all nine to be guilty. One of them received a sentence of life imprisonment; the other eight were given the death penalty. Many American citizens were shocked by the proceedings of the trial and considered it a miscarriage of justice. Yet most black organizations, including the NAACP, felt that they had to be careful when it came to aiding the convicted youths. The one group that became outspoken in its efforts to defend the youths was the Communist party.

The convicted youths in the Scottsboro case at the Jefferson, Alabama, jail around the time when they were visited by Hughes.

Hughes was given an excellent opportunity to express his political views when he was told that he would be granted a fellowship of $1,000 from the Julius Rosenwald Fund simply if he applied for it. Hughes drafted a proposal, outlining his plan for a poetry-reading tour through the South "to create an interest in racial expression through books and to do what I can to encourage young black literary talent among our people." His proposal was approved, and he used part of the grant to purchase a car to take him from place to place. He used another part of the grant to establish a small publishing company called Golden Stair Press.

Hughes's aim was to publish inexpensive, attractive paperback editions of his poems to be sold to his audiences in the South. Called *The Negro Mother and Other Dramatic Recitations*, these volumes of verse did not contain the fiery and radical poems Hughes was sending to *New Masses*. *The Negro Mother* contained softer poems that would not offend a conservative and religious black audience. Hughes knew that he could not overwhelm his southern audience with fury; rather, he had to seduce them with sentiment and charm. He also commissioned his New York publisher to print a cheaper, one-dollar edition of his earlier collection, *The Weary Blues*, which he took with him to the South.

Hughes left for his tour on November 2, 1931, from the 135th Street YMCA in Harlem—the same place he had stayed 10 years earlier, when he first came to New York. His car was filled with books and posters advertising the tour and was driven by Radcliffe Lucas, a friend from Lincoln University. Their first stop, at a black trade school in Philadelphia, was followed by stops at several black colleges in Virginia.

In undertaking this journey, Hughes was not indulging in a pleasure trip but embarking on a literary and political campaign "by taking poetry, my poetry,

"I've never had a finer response anywhere, or met more beautiful people," Hughes said during his first reading tour of the South.

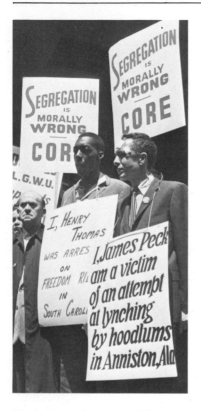

Hughes's reading tour of the South, which began in November 1931, took place during a time when there were numerous incidents of racial violence. Such incidents continued to take place in the South, as is evidenced by this scene from 1961.

to *my* people." His purpose put him in danger of physical violence, for the South in the early 1930s was a particularly dangerous place for blacks.

During the first weekend of Hughes's tour, two unfortunate racial incidents occurred in the South. In one of the incidents, the football coach of Alabama A & M Institute in Normal, Alabama, was beaten to death after mistakenly parking his car in a "white" parking lot while attending a football game. In the other incident, Julia Derricotte, dean of women at Fisk University in Nashville, Tennessee, died after she was refused admission to a whites-only hospital following a car accident.

One of the more controversial stops on Hughes's tour was made at the University of North Carolina at Chapel Hill. Hughes was invited to lecture there by two students who were members of the local chapter of the John Reed Club. These students published a leftist campus newspaper called *Contempo*, and they released an issue of the newspaper, featuring a militant poem that Hughes had sent them, to coincide with his arrival on campus. The poem, entitled "Christ in Alabama," contains provocative language and a harsh commentary on southern justice and race relations. The publication of the poem, which concludes with the lines "Nigger Christ/On the cross of the South," touched off a furor not only in Chapel Hill but throughout the South. Hughes had to receive police protection while he held a reading at the University of North Carolina.

The commotion at Chapel Hill gave Hughes's tour a publicity boost, yet the tour had been well received even before Hughes reached North Carolina. His stock of The Negro Mother sold out only a week after he left New York, and more copies had to be shipped to him. Proceeding through South Carolina, Georgia, and Florida, Hughes usually ended his readings with "I, Too, Sing America," the poem he had written while he was stranded in Genoa, Italy.

Hughes pushed the tour at an exhausting pace through Alabama, where he visited the young men convicted in the Scottsboro case in their prison cells on death row. He then went on to Tennessee, Missouri, Kansas, and Oklahoma. After taking a short break to return to New York in March 1932, he resumed the tour in Texas and continued on to New Mexico, Arizona, and California. He ended the tour in San Francisco, where he rested as a guest in the home of a wealthy admirer, Noel Sullivan.

While Hughes was in California, he received a telegram from his friend and former typist, Louise Thompson. The two had discussed work on a movie about American blacks while he had been in New York back in March. The movie was to be filmed in the Soviet Union and financed by the Soviet film company Meschrabpom. The making of the film had been approved by the Soviet government. Thompson's telegram read that the participants in the project—including Hughes, who was to work on the script—were to assemble in New York and then sail to Russia in June. "This unexpected chance to work in films in Russia seemed to open a new door to me," Hughes said. "At that time Hollywood did not employ Negro writers."

The Kremlin, the seat of the Soviet government, in Moscow, a city where Hughes felt he was able to participate in society without encountering racial oppression.

Hughes's first stop in the Soviet Union was Leningrad, formerly the capital of the Russian empire when the city was known as St. Petersburg. The summer palace of Peter the Great is shown here.

Hughes and a group of 21 other members of the film project arrived in Leningrad on June 25, 1932. They checked into the Hotel Metropole in Moscow 10 days later and began work on the film, called *Black and White*, 2 months after that. Directed by an inexperienced German filmmaker, the film had a script that appeared to Hughes to have been written in Russian by a committee of bureaucrats who had no knowledge of how people really lived in the United States. When a poorly translated version of the script reached Hughes, he was astonished to find that the plot outline called for black steelworkers in the South to appeal to their rich black friend in Birmingham, Alabama, to send a message for help against racism on their private radio station. This appeal for help was directed to the white steelworker comrades in the North. A typical scene in the script depicted the son of a wealthy white southern industrialist dancing at a party in his father's house with a young black maid.

The project had other problems besides the poor screenplay. Most of the group of actors from New York were amateurs who were unfamiliar with southern blues and work songs. No sets had been built. No costumes had been made. And no contract between the company and any members of Hughes's group had been signed. By August, when shooting should have been well under way, the project collapsed in disarray and confusion.

As compensation for the failed project, the American group was offered a chance by the Russian film company to go on a tour of the country in September. Hughes toured central Asia, intending to write a series of articles for the Soviet newspaper *Izvestia* on the treatment of ethnic minorities in the Soviet Union. On the steppes of Turkistan, Hughes met Arthur Koestler, a journalist who was to become famous for his myth-shattering book about communism, *Darkness at Noon*. The two reporters traveled together for some time, sharing their observations of Russian society.

Hughes had arrived in the Soviet Union feeling sympathy for the people and their leadership, who were trying to solve many political and social problems. Like many artists and intellectuals of the 1930s, he saw the Soviet system as a symbol of hope and as a model for action. Even though the communist government had then been in power for only 15 years and the country was still undeniably poor, he felt that

A statue of Communist leader V. I. Lenin is unveiled before the Soviet people, who impressed Hughes by holding writers in great esteem.

Hughes's tour of central Asia in 1932 allowed him to compare the treatment of ethnic minorities in the Soviet Union with the treatment of blacks in the American South.

much progress in their society had been made. For one thing, Hughes did not see any obvious signs of racism. Class and racial barriers were being attacked, literacy programs were being initiated, and free medical clinics were being established for all. These were far greater improvements than those Hughes saw taking place in his own country, where a record number of people were without jobs and were close to starvation. Everyone he saw in the Soviet Union seemed to be working, and he was impressed. What he did not see, or refused to see, were other problems created by the Soviet system: the labor camps, the arrest of anyone who disagreed with the state, or the corruption of party officials.

Hughes's tour of Russia lasted until January, when the group returned to Moscow. Most of the remaining members of the film project then returned to the United States. But with the depression there growing worse, Hughes decided to remain abroad, writing bold poetry and more conventional short stories. Some of the poems were eventually published in *New Masses*, but when Hughes later tried to publish a collection of them in a book entitled *Good Morning, Revolution*, he was unsuccessful. Even his friend and chief publishing ally, Carl Van Vechten, thought the work too radical to gain much acceptance in the United States.

During Hughes's last few months in Russia, he was reintroduced to Sylvia Chen, a Moscow-based dancer of Chinese ancestry whom he had met the previous fall in Harlem. Before long, the two of them began to talk about getting married. The marriage never took place, but Hughes felt so strongly about Sylvia Chen that marriage was a subject he continued to discuss in letters with her even after he returned to the United States.

Hughes finally left Russia in June 1933, traveling on the Trans-Siberian railroad to Vladivostok. From there he journeyed to Japan, took a side trip to Shanghai in China (where he was invited to dinner with Madame Sun Yat-sen, the widow of the great Chinese statesman), and finally sailed across the Pacific for the United States. He landed in San Francisco in early August.

Within a year's time, Hughes had traveled completely around the world. ☙

A literary circle in central Asia: Hughes with (from left to right) Ukrainian writer Kolya Shagurin; president of the Turkoman Writers Federation Shaarieh Kikilov; and Hungarian-born British writer Arthur Koestler.

8

TRAVELS
AND
TRAVAILS

WHILE HUGHES was in Russia, he had developed the idea of writing a series of short stories whose most important theme would be the relationship between blacks and whites. However, he had returned to the United States with almost no money, so finding the time to work on the project seemed to be a concern. He had to figure out a way of making a living.

Hughes's friend Noel Sullivan solved this problem in one stroke. He offered the 31-year-old poet the use of his second house, called Ennesfree, which was located in the quaint seaside hamlet of Carmel-by-the-Sea, several hours south of San Francisco. Hughes accepted this offer at once. He liked Sullivan and sensed that as a patron Sullivan, unlike Charlotte Mason, would leave him alone with his work.

Ennesfree was a light and airy, two-bedroom cottage with a view of the Pacific Ocean. Hughes was allowed to live there rent free, with Sullivan providing for his food and a cook. The village of Carmel, which then consisted of around a thousand people, had been conceived as an artists' colony in the late 19th century. By 1933 a number of painters, writers, and photographers still lived there, but it had also become a retirement community for the wealthy.

"The nearest I've ever come to la vie de bohème [the bohemian life] was my winter in Mexico when my friends were almost all writers and artists," Hughes said of his last visit to the country.

American journalist and poet
John Reed helped to organize the
Communist Labor party in the
United States. Hughes joined the
local chapter of the John Reed
Club in 1933, while he was living
in Carmel, California.

Hughes was welcomed as an honored guest by the artists who lived in Carmel, among them the former muckraking journalist Lincoln Steffens, the photographer Edward Weston, and the sculptor Jo Davidson. Most of the Carmel artists belonged to the local chapter of the John Reed Club, and Hughes joined them. He also started to work on some short stories. Many of these touched on the relationships between blacks and whites. Hughes's literary agent, Max Lieber, worked hard to place these stories in major magazines, but he met with only limited success. Lieber was told that the stories were too shocking. Americans in the midst of the depression wanted to read about subjects that would make them forget their problems rather than dwell on subjects that would not go away.

Despite being unable to find an audience for Hughes's work, Lieber encouraged him to continue with his writing. By December 1933 Hughes had written enough of these stories for a book-length collection. He sent them to Carl Van Vechten in New York, who liked them and helped to get them published in 1934 under the title *The Ways of White Folks*.

The gritty, ironic stories collected in *The Ways of White Folks* were well received, although a few critics bristled over Hughes's representation of patronizing white liberals. The acclaim for *The Ways of White Folks* cheered Hughes. He said that this was "the first long period in my life when I was able, unworried and unhurried, to stay quietly in one place and devote myself to writing," and it proved that with such devotion he could be successful.

Through the Carmel John Reed Club, Hughes became active in 1934 in farmworkers' strikes and in a longshoremen's strike. The longshoremen's strike in San Francisco was a particularly bloody and disruptive affair. The California media soon began accusing the strikers and their supporters of being Communists whose real goal was to overthrow the government. The local Carmel newspaper subsequently began putting pressure on the John Reed Club. Calls for the police to hold and question club members began to appear in print, and in July 1934 an American Legion post was formed to counter what was perceived as the "menace" of the John Reed Club. Hughes, the only black member of the Carmel branch, was singled out for attack, with one newspaper calling him "a tireless advocator for Soviet Rule, for Communism in this country." With the situation in Carmel becoming increasingly hostile, Hughes decided to leave Ennesfree for the relative safety of San Francisco.

Throughout this period of controversy, Hughes kept to his work schedule. He collaborated with Lincoln Steffens's wife, Ella Winter, on a play called *Blood on the Fields*, based on the agricultural strikes in California. He worked on the memoirs of his journey to the Soviet Union, which he titled *From Harlem to Samarkand*. And he wrote a few poems in the

This riot scene shows the hostilities that were present during the San Francisco longshoremen's strike in 1934. As a member of the John Reed Club, Hughes was treated as though he were a Communist siding with the strikers.

A mural by the Mexican painter Diego Rivera covers a wall at the Ministry of Education in Mexico City. Hughes befriended a number of Mexican artists—including Rivera—during the poet's three visits south of the United States border.

ultramilitant style he had developed when he was in the Soviet Union, including "One More 'S' in the U.S.A.," a verse read to the eighth convention of the U.S. Communist Party in 1934:

> Put one more S in the U.S.A.
> To make it Soviet.
> One more S in the U.S.A.
> Oh, we'll live to see it yet.
> When the land belongs to the farmers
> And the factories to the working men—
> The U.S.A. when we take control
> Will be the U.S.S.A. then . . .

Before long, he was asked to head the Communist party's major black organization, the League of Struggle for Negro Rights.

Despite Hughes's productivity, he was having some trouble with his career as a writer. Even with its excellent reviews, *The Ways of White Folks* did not sell well. Max Lieber had a hard time placing Hughes's stories in magazines. Knopf, his New York publisher, rejected *From Harlem to Samarkand*. And *Blood on the Fields* was turned down by the Theater Union of New York, a group Hughes had hoped would produce the play.

Feeling that he had reached yet another low point in his life, Hughes decided that it was once again time to move on. He left California for Reno, Nevada, where he found a cheap room in Reno's small black ghetto. With his bank account overdrawn and his writing failing to find an audience, he informed Lieber about a scheme he was attempting out of desperation: he had begun writing sentimental short stories that featured only conventional white characters. Writing under the pseudonym of David Boatman, Hughes would try to pass himself off as a white author. He never got the chance to carry out this scheme completely, however. Several weeks after he started writing stories as David Boatman, he learned that his father had died in Mexico.

Borrowing $150 from his New York publisher and cashing a check from *Esquire* magazine for one of the few stories he had managed to have published, Hughes headed south in December 1934 to pay his last respects to his father and settle the estate he had left. Hughes had not seen his father since 1921, and they had exchanged few letters in the intervening years. Yet James Hughes had always managed to have a powerful hold on his son's psyche, and his death gave Langston a sense of release.

Hughes stayed in Mexico City with his father's longtime friends, the three Patiño sisters, who had

In paintings such as the one shown here, Diego Rivera reflected his native culture and the lives of the Mexican people. Rivera's art inspired Hughes to seek a similar portrayal of the black experience in his own work.

This portrait of Hughes was taken by the French photographer Henri Cartier-Bresson. The two friends briefly shared an apartment in Mexico City in 1935.

been willed James Hughes's entire estate. The sisters insisted that Hughes take a quarter of the estate for himself. After initially resisting their offer, he accepted a portion of the small amount of cash left in his father's bank account.

Jose Antonio Fernández de Castro, Hughes's friend from Cuba who had become a translator of Hughes's work, was living in Mexico City at that time as a consular officer at the Cuban embassy. Hughes reestablished his friendship with Fernández de Castro as well as with Miguel Covarrubias, the illustrator of Hughes's first book *The Weary Blues*, soon after his 33rd birthday. Within weeks of their reunion, Hughes slipped comfortably into the bohemian life of Mexico City. In March he left the Patiño sisters' house to share an apartment with a new friend, the young French photographer Henri Cartier-Bresson.

Hughes stayed in Mexico City until June, leading the life of a famous expatriate while coming to grips with the sense of freedom he felt after his father's death. He then left Mexico to visit his mother, who was living in Oberlin, Ohio. On his way to visit her, he stopped off in Los Angeles, where he stayed with an old friend from New York, Arna Bontemps. Hughes decided to spend the summer collaborating with Bontemps on a children's book, *Paste Board Bandits*, based on tales Hughes had heard over the years in Mexico. Despite his friend Wallace Thurman's unsuccessful experience in Hollywood, Hughes also tried to break into the lucrative screenwriting trade. Like Thurman, he had little success. Hollywood was not in the habit of employing black writers.

While Hughes was in Mexico, he was chosen to receive a Guggenheim Foundation grant. The Guggenheim fellowship is one of the most prestigious grants given to American artists and writers. The choice of Hughes as a recipient showed that, despite his recent problems in publishing his work, his reputation as a writer was still intact. He was to receive a $1500 grant to work on a novel about urban black life.

Hughes labored fitfully for a year on the novel, but he felt that his inspiration for this work was missing. Instead, he turned his attention to the theatre.

Mulatto, a play he had written in 1930, resurfaced thanks to John Rumsey, Hughes's theatrical agent. Rumsey had found a wealthy, young producer-director named Martin Jones who wanted to produce *Mulatto* on Broadway in New York. Hughes agreed to let Jones develop *Mulatto*, but he soon lost control of his work. Instead of developing Hughes's play as a serious exploration about a mulatto (a person with mixed black and white ancestry), Jones sensationalized the play. He created a piece of commercial theater featuring much sex but little in the way of coherent plot or character development. *Mulatto* opened in October 1935 to good notices for the actors but dreadful reviews for Hughes, including one from the New York *World-Telegram*, calling *Mulatto* "not a play [but] an attempt to dramatize an inferiority complex." Most reviewers seemed unaware that Jones had virtually rewritten the play.

Hughes had more success on a smaller scale with two plays produced by the Gilpin Players in Cleveland in 1936. One of the plays, *Troubled Island*, was the revision of the singing play Hughes began on his trip to Cuba in 1930. The other, *Joy to My Soul*, was a farce he wrote in 1936 while he was working in Cleveland with the Gilpin Players. Perhaps as a result of Martin Jones's instincts for commercialization, *Mulatto* became a hit, and by 1937 Hughes began receiving fairly large royalty checks. Although these royalties may have provided him with some consolation, Hughes still foundered in his art. He wrote few poems of note, and though he occasionally sold a few stories, the income he earned from these stories

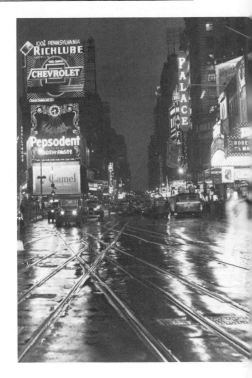

Several of Hughes's plays, including Mulatto *in 1935, have been produced in New York's theater district known as Broadway.*

was not enough to let him support himself. Once again, he felt a trip was necessary for him to reestablish his work.

In July 1937 Hughes returned to Paris for the first time since his days at the Grand Duc. Europe in 1937 was a much more somber place than it had been in 1924. Spain was entering the second year of a civil war, and events elsewhere in Europe seemed to indicate that a full-scale war was close at hand for the rest of the continent.

In Paris, the music still blew all night at the jazz clubs, and Hughes's friend Bricktop had become a big star. Yet the frantic nightlife betrayed a sense of desperation, not joy. Like the United States, Europe had been ravaged by economic depression.

While Hughes was in Paris, he spent several weeks as a delegate to the International Writers' Congress. Invited to the congress by the French writer André Malraux, among others, Hughes joined his fellow writers at the congress in a protest of fascist attempts to overthrow the Republican government in the civil war in Spain. During one of the meetings of the

During the Spanish civil war, Hughes worked as a journalist, interviewing members of the Lincoln Brigade, the American volunteer force siding with the Loyalist cause. This group of fighters is shown as they return to America in 1939.

congress, Hughes told the audience, "In America, Negroes do not have to be told what fascism is in action. We know. Its theories of Nordic supremacy and economic suppression have long been realities to us."

Among the writers attending the congress were Nicolás Guillén and Jacques Roumain. Both men had become Communists since Hughes had last seen them, and both had served time in prison in their respective countries. After the conference ended, Hughes and Guillén, who had become a journalist, traveled to Spain to help the Republicans in their civil war. Hughes worked there as a reporter for the Associated Press and the Baltimore *Afro-American* for six months. He made a number of visits to the battlefront and interviewed black members of the Lincoln Brigade, the American volunteer force siding with the Republican army. He also worked as a reporter and press aide for the Alianza di Intelectuales Antifascistas (Alliance of Antifascist Intellectuals), a public relations and propaganda bureau made up of writers and artists. Through the Alianza he met several notable Americans who were helping the Republican cause, including Ernest Hemingway, Lillian Hellman, and Dorothy Parker. He also reencountered Louise Thompson.

The tragic suffering of the Spanish people during this bloody civil war sparked Hughes's creative imagination in such poems as "Madrid, 1937." These poems, although political-minded, were not as radical as the ones he had written after visiting Russia only four years before. The pressure of having to live off his literary wits had mellowed him somewhat. Hughes had begun to realize that there was little point in fighting the conservative forces in America as relentlessly as he had been doing. If he was to live and work, some adjustment in his approach to writing had to be made. ❧

Ernest Hemingway returns to America after reporting on the civil war in Spain. "I found him a big likable fellow," Hughes said of the famous writer.

HARLEM SUITCASE THEATRE OPENS ITS SECOND SEASON

(Sponsored By Lodge 691, International Workers Order)

SUNDAY, OCTOBER 30th, 9 P. M.

I.W.O. COMMUNITY CENTER, 317 WEST 125th STREET

●

HILARIOUS HISTRIONICS IN FIVE SCENES

FROM UNCLE TOM'S CABIN TO
EM-FUEHRER JONES

OR

THE TABLES TURNED

S

"One Pancake To Another"

"I Am The Law—For Three"

INCLUDING

LIMITATIONS OF LIFE

And

JERSEY CITY JUSTICE

E

"Joe Kayoe Hitler"

Above All

AS PRESENTED BY THE ART AND ARTISTS OF
THE HARLEM SUITCASE THEATRE

E

"Little Eva's End"

A Series of Pre-views of skits for a Revue Written by the Theatre Staff

AND

DON'T YOU WANT TO BE FREE?

A POETIC DRAMA BY LANGSTON HUGHES AND DIRECTED BY HILARY PHILLIPS

Regular Performances of this Double Bill Every Sunday Throughout November

Maintaining Our Popular Admission Price of 35c

●

Forthcoming Productions:

YOUNG MAN OF HARLEM, by Powell Lindsay

FUENTE OVEJUNA Adapted by Dorothy Peterson and Langston Hughes from the Spanish of Lope de Vega

FRONT PORCH, by Langston Hughes

ORGANIZER, A folk opera Libretto by Langston Hughes. Music by James P. Johnson.

9

THE
WANDERING
POET

AFTER VISITING THE battlefields of Spain, Hughes decided to write real-life dramas "that will be equal to anybody's battlefront." He returned to New York in early 1938 and began to write and produce plays for the Harlem Suitcase Theater, which he cofounded with Louise Thompson. Borrowing some of the revolutionary techniques he had seen in Russian theater, Hughes wrote and then directed the most remarkable theatrical work of his career, *Don't You Want to Be Free?* Performed on a bare stage, the play is a montage of sermons, dramatic vignettes, poetry, exhortations, and blues songs. *Don't You Want to Be Free?* captured the imagination of its audience and played to capacity crowds until the end of the Suitcase Theater's first season.

In 1939 Hughes returned to Los Angeles. Arna Bontemps had interested the black film actor and musician Clarence Muse in adapting one of Bontemps's novels, *God Sends Sunday*, into a film script. Hughes was asked to join the project as a scriptwriter. The film, which was retitled *Way Down South*, was also reworked by its producer, Sol Lesser. Hughes found working in Hollywood to be a humiliating experience. "Hollywood," he said, "has spread in exaggerated form every ugly and ridiculous stereotype of the deep South's conception of Negro characters." While he was there he earned more money on a

Adolf Hitler and Nazi Germany became the targets of Hughes's literary wit when he joined the Writers War Board in 1942 to spur on the American war effort.

consistent basis than he had ever before, but his employment as a scriptwriter did not last for long. Once *Way Down South* was completed, Hughes was not offered any more film work.

Hughes spent the early part of 1940 working on his autobiography, *The Big Sea*, which tells in brilliantly clear language the story of his life up to the year 1931. One of his most successful efforts at prose writing, *The Big Sea* won generally favorable reviews, although its sales were disappointingly small.

After writing plays, film scripts, and prose, Hughes returned to writing poetry and going on reading tours. In 1942 he returned to Harlem, splitting the rent on an apartment with his childhood friends Emerson and Toy Harper. He maintained a share of an apartment in Harlem for the rest of his life.

Although Hughes had clearly tempered his left-wing radicalism by the early 1940s, he remained as committed as ever to his ideals of social justice and racial equality. Consequently, he eagerly helped with the American war effort when the United States entered World War II in December 1941. He joined the Writers War Board, penning articles for army newspapers, composing lyrics with W. C. Handy and Clarence Muse for war blues to be sung at rallies, and thinking up jingles to spur on the troops along with jingles to combat segregation, such as "Look like by now/Folks ought to know/It's hard to beat Hitler/Protecting Jim Crow."

Hughes's contribution to American literature began to be recognized by more and more people after the war was over. He was appointed poet-in-residence at Atlanta University in 1947 and held a position as poet-teacher at the University of Chicago in 1949. He also translated into English works written by his friends, including Jacques Roumain and Nicolás Guillén, among others. His opera libretto, *Troubled Island*,

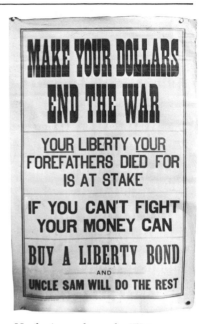

Hughes's work on the Writers War Board enabled a large segment of the American public to sample his talents.

was performed by the New York City Opera Company on March 31, 1949. Leopold Stokowski called it "one of the most inspired expressions of Negro art in the United States."

Among Hughes's most important works of this time was a long-term project that he began in 1943. He created a character named Jesse B. Semple and made him the focus of dozens of short stories. These stories were written originally as part of a regular column for *The Chicago Defender*, a weekly black newspaper, before appearing regularly in the *New York Post*. Collected in four books, the stories chronicled the highs and lows, the frustrations and triumphs, of an Afro-American Everyman, Jesse Semple (also known as Simple). The stories capture the essence of Hughes's personality: his wit, his humor, and his generosity of spirit. "The character of My Simple-Minded Friend is really very simple," he said. "It is just myself talking to me."

The jazz style known as bebop, featuring abrupt accents and unusual rhythms, began to take Harlem by storm around 1940. These accents and rhythms were soon captured by Hughes in his poetry collection Montage of a Dream Deferred.

Jesse Semple does not seem to be a fighter. He does not directly challenge racist obstacles. However, he does confront the problems of everyday life with humor and quiet determination. During Hughes's lifetime, the Semple stories became his most popular work among blacks, and he wrote them for 23 years.

Hughes's most ambitious poetry collection, *Montage of a Dream Deferred*, was published in 1951. As the title indicates, this volume of poems makes use of the startling montage technique Hughes first incorporated in his play *Don't You Want to Be Free?* It presents a series of images from everyday life in Harlem as seen by the poet. Although the poems may seem to have been arranged at random, Hughes meant the collection to be viewed as a united narrative. The montage of poems takes the reader through one complete day and night in Harlem.

In some of these poems, Hughes uses a writing style to mirror be-bop, the new jazz style that had just appeared in Harlem. But no matter what the writing style of the poems are in *Montage of a Dream Deferred*, Hughes tackles the problem of being black in America. In "Harlem," the most famous poem in the collection, he asks:

Although known chiefly as a poet, Hughes also wrote librettos for several operas.

> What happens to a dream deferred?
> Does it dry up
> like a raisin in the sun?
>
> Or fester like a sore—
> And then run?
> Does it stink like rotten meat?
> Or crust and sugar over—
> Like syrupy sweet?
>
> Maybe it just sags
> like a heavy load.
>
> Or does it explode?

Hughes testifies about his radical past before the McCarthy Committee in March 1953.

During the time he was preparing *Montage of a Dream Deferred* for publication, Hughes's name began to appear in testimonies being given before congressional committees investigating on the influence of communism in the United States. These investigations occurred during a time when anti-Communist feelings in the United States had turned into a nationwide hysteria. Many loyal citizens found their reputations sullied by false accusations or misleading statements that they were Communists. Such accusations were presented before both the Senate committee headed by Joseph McCarthy, a senator from Wisconsin, and the House Un-American Activities Committee. On March 26, 1953, Hughes was finally called to come before the McCarthy committee. His pro-Communist sympathies were well known and documented in his writings. In a deal arranged before he gave his testimony, Hughes agreed to cooperate with the committee by admitting his past radicalism and his prior association with groups allied with the Communist party. In exchange for this admission, he did not have to name specific persons as collaborators. This arrangement was a relatively lenient one for Hughes. Many witnesses before the committee were either jailed when they refused to testify or were coerced into publicly accusing their former friends and colleagues. Other people called to come before the committee, such as Hughes's literary agent, Max Lieber, fled the country in order to avoid giving testimony.

Although no charges of any kind were ever filed against Hughes, and although he had committed no crime—unless speaking one's conscience is considered a crime—his overall character was called into question by the committee. A number of groups canceled Hughes's appearances on his reading tours, and some of his readings were picketed. For a while, these cancellations affected Hughes's ability to earn a living.

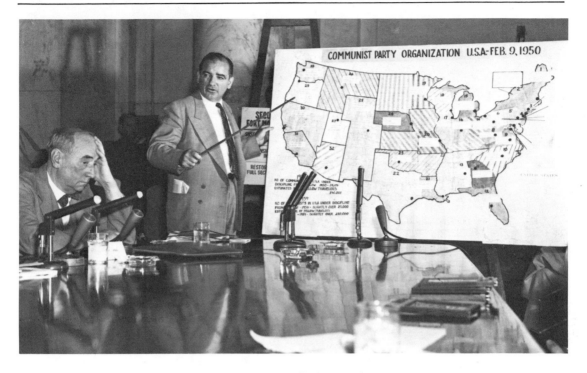

COMMUNIST PARTY ORGANIZATION U.S.A.-FEB. 9, 1950

Nonetheless, Hughes persevered. He collaborated with photographer Roy de Carava in *Sweet Flypaper of Life* (1955) and with Milton Meltzer in *A Pictorial History of the Negro People in America* (1955), doing research and writing for both projects. *I Wonder As I Wander*, the second of his autobiographies, was published during this time. In this volume Hughes wrote about the people and events of his life up until 1938. In 1959 a retrospective of 40 years of his poetry was published in *Selected Poems*. Although the poems in this collection, all chosen by Hughes, include most of the major poems of his career, it is significant to note some of the poems that Hughes chose to leave out. None of his militant verses from the 1930s are included, nor are many of his scathing poems mocking religion and American justice. In seeking to gain respectability, Hughes stopped being so politically—but not racially—militant. By omitting some important poems, such as "Advertisement for the Waldorf-

Senator Joseph McCarthy conducts a Senate committee hearing on the influence of Communism in America by using a map of the country to illustrate the growth of the Communist party in American society.

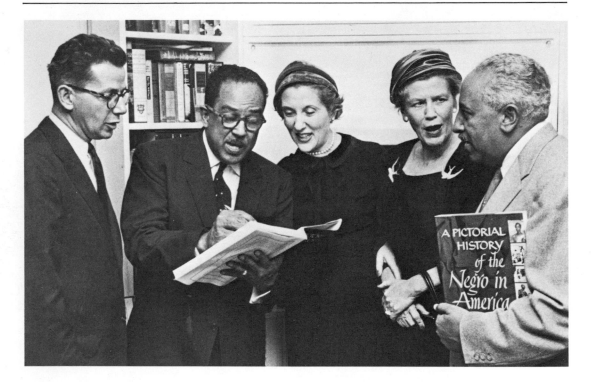

Hughes and coauthor Milton Meltzer (left) autograph copies of their book A Pictorial History of the Negro in America. *Writer Arna Bontemps holds a copy of the book (at right).*

Astoria" and "Christ in Alabama," he in effect rewrote his personal and professional history for a generation of readers.

In the last decade of Hughes's life, he devoted much of his energy to reviewing the fiction of young black writers, including the novelist James Baldwin and the poet Gwendolyn Brooks. Hughes also became involved with the government as a spokesman for American culture. Such involvement was made possible by the relatively liberal administrations of Presidents John F. Kennedy and Lyndon Johnson in the 1960s. He visited Europe and Africa several times as an official cultural emissary of the U.S. State Department.

Hughes also continued to write plays in the 1960s, but these productions met with little commercial success. In two of them, *Gospel Glow* and *Tambourines to Glory*, Hughes attempted to bring to the stage dramatic interpretations of black religion as experienced through gospel music. He believed that gospel music was an important folk tradition in Afro-American culture, and he thought its intense emotional experience could be successfully transformed into powerful theater. In spite of some favorable reviews, these two plays had short runs in New York's off-Broadway theaters in 1962 and 1963, respectively.

Hughes's health began to fail in the spring of 1967. When he experienced an undiagnosed physical attack so severe that it made him fear for his life, he checked into a public hospital under his given name, James Hughes. He remained in the hospital for three weeks. After an operation on his prostate gland on May 19, his condition worsened, and he died on May 22, 1967, at the age of 65. His funeral was held, in accordance with the instructions in his will, in a Harlem funeral home, not in a church. According to his request, a jazz band was hired to celebrate, rather than mourn, his memory.

By the time of Hughes's death, he had already been honored by many universities and institutions, including the Library of Congress, as the guiding light of black literature around the world. From Nicolás Guillén and Jacques Roumain to Alice Walker and Imamu Amiri Baraka, Hughes showed black writers the importance of writing about racial freedom. In return, he saw blacks in America fight to improve society and blacks in Africa seek to liberate themselves from European rule. These twin movements toward freedom derived their inspiration in no small part from the efforts of Langston Hughes, who in the long years since he had crossed the Mississippi bridge at St. Louis had become the poet laureate of the black world. •◌•

Hughes received an award in 1962 for being an exceptional innovator in the literary arts.

CHRONOLOGY

February 1, 1902	Born James Langston Hughes in Joplin, Missouri
1916	Moves to Cleveland, Ohio; attends Central High School
1919	Travels with his father to Toluca, Mexico
June 1920	Graduates from high school
July 1920	Writes "The Negro Speaks of Rivers"
1920	Visits his father in Mexico; publishes his first poem in *Brownies' Book*
September 4, 1921	Arrives in New York City; begins his studies at Columbia University
May 1922	Leaves Columbia
1922	Works as a crewman on the *Oronoke*, anchored at Jones Point, New York
March 1923	Writes "The Weary Blues"
1923	Ships out for Africa on the *West Hesseltine*
February 1924	Ships out for the Netherlands; jumps ship at Rotterdam and travels to Paris
1924	Writes "I, Too, Sing America"
1925	Moves to Washington, D.C.; works for Dr. Carter Woodson; meets Carl Van Vechten
May 1925	"The Weary Blues" wins poetry contest
November 1925	Hughes is "discovered" by Vachel Lindsay
January 1926	*The Weary Blues* is published
February 1926	Hughes enters Lincoln University
1927	*Fine Clothes to the Jew* is published; meets Charlotte Mason; travels to the South on first poetry reading tour
1929	Graduates from Lincoln University
February 1930	Travels to Cuba
1930	Mason breaks off her patronage relationship with Hughes
1931	Hughes visits Cuba and Haiti; begins reading tour of the United States
1932	Works in the Soviet Union on film project; travels as a reporter for *Izvestia*
1933	Lives and works in Carmel, California
1934	Father dies; Hughes travels to Mexico City
October 24, 1935	*Mulatto* opens on Broadway
July 1937	Hughes travels to Paris; covers the Spanish Civil War as a reporter
June 1938	Mother dies
1938	Hughes founds Harlem Suitcase Theater; writes and directs *Don't You Want to Be Free?*

1939	Works in Los Angeles on *Way Down South*
1940	*The Big Sea* is published
1942	Hughes works for the Writers War Board
1943	Begins writing Semple stories for a newspaper column
1947	Appointed poet-in-residence at Atlanta University
1951	*Montage of a Dream Deferred* is published
March 26, 1953	Hughes subpoenaed to testify before McCarthy committee
1956	*I Wonder as I Wander* is published
1959	*Selected Poems* is published
1960–63	Hughes travels to Europe and Africa as cultural emissary for U. S. State Department
May 22, 1967	Dies in New York City

FURTHER READING

————— ✿ —————

Berry, Faith. *Langston Hughes: Before and Beyond Harlem.* Connecticut: Lawrence Hill & Company, 1983.

Huggins, Nathan. *Voices from the Harlem Renaissance.* New York: Oxford University Press, 1976.

Hughes, Langston. *The Big Sea.* New York: Alfred A. Knopf, 1940.

————. *I Wonder As I Wander.* New York: Rhinehart, 1956.

————. *Selected Poetry of Langston Hughes.* New York: Alfred A. Knopf, 1959.

Rampersad, Arnold. *The Life of Langston Hughes: I, Too, Sing America.* Volume 1. New York: Oxford University Press, 1986.

INDEX

PHOTO CREDITS

JACK RUMMEL is a free-lance writer who has written articles about Latin America and the South and has followed the development of Gulf-Coast blues for the past 20 years. Mr. Rummel currently lives in Hoboken, New Jersey.